TEACHING *for* TOMORROW

TEACHING *for* TOMORROW

Teaching
Content
<u>and</u>
Problem-
Solving
Skills

Ted McCain

Foreword by Frank S. Kelly

CORWIN PRESS
A Sage Publications Company
Thousand Oaks, California

For information:

Corwin Press
A Sage Publications Company
2455 Teller Road
Thousand Oaks, California 91320
www.corwinpress.com

Sage Publications Ltd.
1 Oliver's Yard
55 City Road
London EC1Y 1SP
United Kingdom

Sage Publications India Pvt. Ltd.
B-42, Panchsheel Enclave
Post Box 4109
New Delhi 110 017 India

Printed in the United States of America.

Library of Congress Cataloging-in-Publication Data

McCain, Ted D. E.
Teaching for tomorrow: Teaching content and problem-solving
skills / Ted McCain.
     p. cm.
Includes bibliographical references and index.
ISBN 978-1-4129-1383-6 (cloth) — ISBN 978-1-4129-1384-3 (pbk.)
     1. High school teaching. 2. Problem-solving—Study and teaching
(Secondary) 3. School-to-work transition. I. Title.
LB1607.M38 2005
373.1102—dc22   2004022982

This book is printed on acid-free paper.

08   09   10   9   8   7   6   5   4

Acquisitions Editor:	Elizabeth Brenkus
Editorial Assistant:	Candice L. Ling
Production Editor:	Laureen A. Shea
Copy Editor:	Meredith L. Brittain
Typesetter:	C&M Digitals (P) Ltd.
Proofreader:	Sally M. Scott
Indexer:	Pamela Van Huss
Cover Designer:	Michael Dubowe
Graphic Designer:	Anthony Paular

Contents

Foreword   vii

Preface   ix

Acknowledgments   xi

About the Author   xiii

1. **What Skills Will Students
   Need for the 21st Century?**   **1**
   How I Discovered I Was a
     "Highly Educated Useless Person"   1
   How I Discovered I Was Producing
     "Highly Educated Useless People"   3
   School Skills   5
   Real-World Skills   7
   "Stand and Deliver" Lecture-Style Teaching   10
   The Myth of Postsecondary Education   13
   It's Time to Rethink How We Teach   14

2. **Six Ways to Teach for
   Independent and Higher Learning**   **17**
   Resisting the Temptation to "Tell"   18
   Providing Context to Content   22
   Fostering Independent Thinking   26
   Moving to Problem Solving   28
     The Shift From Telling to Discovery   31
     Transforming Your
       Curriculum With Real-World Role Play   34
     The Role of Technology
       in Teaching for Tomorrow   35

Progressively Withdrawing From
  Helping Students   39
    The Fear of Failure   40
  Reevaluating Evaluation   44

3. Teaching Students How to Solve Problems   49
  The 4 Ds of Problem Solving   50
    Step One: Define   51
    Step Two: Design   57
    Step Three: Do   63
    Step Four: Debrief   64
  Teacher Evaluation of Process Skills   67
    Time Management   68
    Project Management   69
    Research   69
    Project Design   70
    Teamwork   72
  Student Evaluation of Process Skills   73
  Putting It All Together   75
  A New Role for Teachers   76
  A New Way to Evaluate   77
    Evaluating the Process   77
    Evaluating Personal Attributes   79
  Making the Transition
    to a New Teaching Approach   82
  Preparing for Success in the 21st Century:
    Problem Solving, Role Playing,
    and Reality Simulation   84

References   87

Index   89

Foreword

It may seem curious that Ted McCain, having written a fine new book to stretch educators' notions about instruction, would turn to an architect to draft the foreword. Because we had worked together on technology-related programs for a number of school districts, Ted asked that I review his final draft. Although the problem-solving, project-based instruction he proposes may seem challenging to K–12 educators, I was, as an architect, instantly comfortable with the concepts because that is how architectural education has worked since the 19th century. But Ted has gone far beyond adapting an old idea to a new context, and there is much to learn here for any educator.

Early in the book, Ted draws a distinction between "school skills" and "real-world skills," worrying that, in the past, his teaching may have been producing "highly educated useless people." It may be helpful in this regard to reflect on why architectural schools have used project-based instruction for so long to bridge this gap. Architecture is less a discipline than an amalgamation of disciplines, and its products are "projects." Creating major buildings in urban environments entails creative, artistic skills, but the process also involves in equal measure engineering and construction skills, political and social skills, business and legal skills, and communication skills (including writing, speaking, and creating graphics). Most architectural problems involve using all these elements together to address clients' functional, aesthetic, budgetary, and schedule issues, which never have simple or singular solutions.

Architecture schools use projects modeled on those from the real world as vehicles for integrating all the skills required. The architecture teacher often involves "clients" from outside the school to help students understand the requirements of the project. Students, each with his or her own work station, study in studios under the guidance of professors who define the problem to be solved but who do not themselves know the potential solutions. Students take conventional core subjects and special courses in history, engineering, business, and graphics, but all are integrated through the studio work. At the end of each project, students present and defend their solution to a "jury" of teachers, clients, and practitioners. As students progress through the years, they maintain portfolios as a record of their work that they carry with them after graduation to demonstrate their capabilities to prospective employers. These graduates are "highly educated, useful people" with skills applicable in the real world.

As you read this book, you will understand why, as an architect, I was immediately attracted to Ted's concepts and was pleased to find that the project-based instruction I had experienced as a student and teacher has been enriched and given life in new areas of education. He maps out changes that teachers must make to use problem-solving, project-based instruction effectively. This revised teaching method will go against the grain of those teachers who want to tell students what they should know and do, and who then test them to see if they retained the information in the short term. Ted's strategy is more effective for long-term content retention and life-skill learning, though; he outlines through the 4 Ds (Define, Design, Do, and Debrief) a methodology for problem solving that is applicable to virtually any field. In the process, he substantially alters the roles of both teachers and students, proposing that teachers focus more on structuring problems that will allow students to discover knowledge for themselves.

By the end of the book, I couldn't decide if I would prefer to be a teacher or a student in Ted's school. And perhaps that is the point—that both the student and the teacher should be engaged in solving problems, that neither should know what solutions might emerge, and that both should be learning and growing in the process. That sounds like a great school. Ted undoubtedly intended his book for K–12 educators, and I will tout it to our school clients. But I will also share it with colleagues in architectural schools, who will find that it provides a fresh alternative approach to their old ways of teaching.

Frank S. Kelly
Fellow of the American Institute of Architects

Preface

What is a complete education? This is a critical question that educators at all levels should ask themselves. It is a question that we need to be asking regularly, because the world of the 21st century is constantly changing.

I view a complete, effective education as having two major components. The first is the *acculturation of an individual*, which involves passing on the accumulated knowledge and wisdom of our society to the next generation. Students begin by learning basic skills, such as reading, so they can explore the wealth of material that documents all human endeavors. The following are elements of a complete education:

- An understanding of history and an appreciation for geography, local as well as global
- Exposure to the languages, customs, and beliefs of other cultures around the world
- An understanding of how government functions at the local, state/province, and federal levels
- A knowledge of the scientific principles of life
- An understanding of the environment and how to care for it
- Skill in mathematical calculation
- The ability to express one's ideas clearly in written and spoken form
- Reading material for reflection and personal enjoyment, including various kinds of literature and poetry
- Exposure to the creative expression of ideas through the visual and performing arts
- Knowledge of how to take care of the body to gain an appreciation for the concepts of healthy living and lifelong physical activity

This content has been the focus of traditional education, and I believe it is still vitally important that we continue to pass on this knowledge in educating the youth of the 21st century. Exposing students to the accumulated wisdom gathered from all human experience richly equips them to become informed, thoughtful citizens able to process the complexities of modern life.

However, acculturation is not the only essential component of a complete education. Of equal importance is the *acquisition of practical problem-solving skills,* which will enable students to successfully apply their learning to real-life situations in the workplace and in their personal lives. To become contributing members of the economy, students need the following:

- An understanding of how business operates
- An awareness of the various roles of workers within an organization
- A knowledge of how to perform the basic tasks of running a company
- Skill in solving real-world problems

The public school system has not done a good job of addressing this second essential component of a complete education. We face a growing problem of the gap between the practical skills students need to succeed in the modern world and those that are actually being taught in school. Consequently, there is increasing pressure on teachers to do a better job of teaching these practical skills.

That brings us face to face with a major issue in education today. Teachers are already overtaxed with all the demands placed upon them; to now say that teachers need to do more to equip students with the practical problem-solving skills needed for the working world will not be greeted warmly by those in the classroom. Is there any way we can combine these two major components of a complete education and kill two birds with one stone? Yes. That is what this book is about—restructuring instruction so that traditional content in all subject areas can be delivered in such a way that students develop the practical problem-solving skills they need.

Acknowledgments

C orwin Press gratefully acknowledges the contributions of the following individuals:

Sara Armstrong
Director
Sara Armstrong Consulting
Berkeley, CA

Michael Burke
Director, District Media and Technology Services
Edina Public Schools
Edina, MN

Guylene Robertson
Assistant Superintendent
Cleveland ISD
Cleveland, TX

David Thornburg
Director
Thornburg Center for Professional Development
Lake Barrington, IL

About the Author

 **Ted McCain** is Coordinator of Instructional Technology for Maple Ridge Secondary School in Vancouver, B.C. He worked for several years in the computer industry as a programmer, salesperson, and consultant before entering the teaching profession. In education, he has been a teacher, administrative assistant, and technology consultant. He also has taught computer networking, graphic design, and desktop publishing for Okanagan College, Kelowna, B.C. He is the author of six books on the future, effective teaching, educational technology, and graphic design.

In 1997, Ted received the Prime Minister's Award for Teaching Excellence. He was nominated for this prestigious Canadian national award for his work in developing a real-world technology curriculum for students in Grades 11 and 12 that prepares them for employment in the areas of multimedia, networking, and Internet publishing directly out of high school. Ted was recognized for his work in creating his "4 Ds" approach to solving problems, his unique use of role playing in the classroom, and his idea of progressive withdrawal as a way to foster independence in his students.

For the past twenty years, Ted has done consulting work for businesses and school districts on effective teaching for the digital generation and the implementation of instructional technology. His clients have included Apple Computer, Microsoft, Aldus, and Toyota, as well as many school districts and educational associations in both the United States and Canada.

In 1995, Ted joined the Thornburg Center for Professional Development in Lake Barrington, Illinois, as an associate director. In this role, Ted has expanded his work as a educational futurist. Ted focuses on the impact that the astounding changes taking place in the world today as a consequence of technological development have on students and learning. He is passionate in his belief that schools must change so they can effectively prepare students for the rest of their lives.

This book is dedicated to my wife

CHAPTER ONE

What Skills Will Students Need for the 21st Century?

What skills will students need after they graduate from high school to be successful in the world of technologically driven change in the 21st century? A major focus in education over the last fifteen years has been to equip students with up-to-date technology skills. However, although such skills are critical for students' success, they are not enough if we want our children to keep up with the job market and if we want our country to remain a leader in the world economy. I believe technology skills are secondary in importance to problem-solving skills. I learned this truth the hard way in my early twenties.

HOW I DISCOVERED I WAS A "HIGHLY EDUCATED USELESS PERSON"

While most people were living in blissful ignorance, the thin edge of the microtechnology wedge was forcing its way into the world in the 1970s. Back then, only a few people were participating in this new wave of technological change. I was one of them. I entered the 21st century about twenty-five years early. I bought an Apple II computer and began creating games and educational programs. I wrote essays using a word processor and

1

printed them on a dot matrix printer long before most people had even considered the possibility. I brought my computer to my university classes and ended up teaching my professors how to use it because they had never seen a microcomputer before. My technology skills made me somewhat of a phenom.

Nearing the end of my fourth year in university, I was targeted for postgraduate work by one of my professors. The school system had placed its stamp of approval on me as one identified for success. I entered a master's degree program in computerized terrain analysis, a completely new field of study at that time, convinced I was going to change the world.

To pay for grad school, I needed to take some time away from my studies to earn money. My supervising professor arranged a job for me at a progressive cartographic company that was interested in exploring the possibility of purchasing a computer to assist in map production. I was hired as a "research cartographer." I was elated to have landed an important position with a recognized firm in my field of study.

The first few months of the job were exciting. Convincing the owner that computers had worthwhile map-making capabilities was not difficult. All I had to do was show the owner the amazing things I had made the computer produce for assignments at university. He was impressed. I was pleased with my powers of persuasion. Then the owner did something that I was completely unprepared for—he said: "OK, it looks like the computer can do what I need it to do, so I want you to tell me which one to buy. You have a budget of $500,000." (This was in 1978, when the smallest computers capable of cartography were room-sized and very expensive.) "Go look at systems in North America and Europe and give me your recommendation in six months." Then he left me on my own.

How did I respond? Sheer panic! This was not a hypothetical problem, a theoretically contrived assignment like those I had done in school with only a letter grade riding on the outcome. This was the real thing, with real money and the success of someone's business riding on my work. And there was no instructor there to guide me to the correct answer. I didn't exactly know how to determine what information I needed or where to start looking. And when I did figure out where to go, I wasn't sure what questions to ask. I embarrassed myself in meetings on both sides of the Atlantic with some very high-powered academics and computer salespeople. There was simply not enough time for me to learn by trial and error the problem-solving skills I needed to get the job done. I made some progress, but certainly nowhere near what I needed to be successful. After feeling my way along for four months, I met with the owner of the cartographic company to give a progress report on my work. The meeting did not go well; the owner was astonished at my lack of progress in determining the best computer system for the company. I was asked to clean out my desk and leave.

I was in shock. I asked myself how this could happen to me. In all my years of schooling, hadn't I been a shining example of what the academic system could produce? If that was the case, then how could it be possible that I didn't have what it took to be a success in my first job related to my field of study? While at school, I had achieved top grades—I had done the research, composed the essays, written the lab reports, performed the math calculations, and created the computer programs. Yet, I was unprepared to face the world. My schooling had let me down. I was a product of a system that focuses on abstract theoretical instruction and information regurgitation testing. I had lots of schooling but little ability in applying my learning. I was a "highly educated useless person," very skilled in doing school-related tasks, but lacking the abilities necessary to solve problems independently in a real-world environment. The fact that I was an academic star and possessed exceptional technological skills didn't amount to a hill of beans when it came to being successful in that job. Now, looking back, it's obvious to me how I should have tackled that problem, but at the time, I was at a loss. Over the years, I have talked to many people about their experience leaving school and getting a job. I have discovered that I am not alone in encountering difficulty making the transition from school to the world of work.

HOW I DISCOVERED I WAS PRODUCING "HIGHLY EDUCATED USELESS PEOPLE"

I have worked with Grade 11 and 12 students for more than twenty years, and one thing that continues to amaze me about the young adults who arrive in my classes is their almost complete lack of ability to work on tasks without guidance from me. They may be

"A" students and possess impressive technology skills, but they have not yet learned to be independent thinkers. When I press them to outline the steps they would take to solve a problem, the overwhelming majority of them have no concept that there could even be a structured process to follow, let alone have the ability to implement that process successfully to find a solution to a problem. What will happen when these students leave the school system and have to make it on their own in the working world? Most of these young people are just like I was—they are "highly educated useless people." After discussions with many teachers around North America, I am convinced this is a common situation. How can we say we have done a good job of preparing students for life if, by the time they have been in school for ten or more years, they still don't know how to solve problems on their own?

This lack of problem-solving ability in students is news to many educators. Many teachers feel that the work that students do in school is relevant and useful for the world in general. But is that true? It is important to stop and examine the kinds of skills students acquire as they pass through our classrooms. Do the assignments and tests we give really develop the higher-level thought and problem-solving skills we believe they do? Are we equipping students with the thinking skills necessary for success in the world outside school? Or are we just teaching skills that will enable students simply to move to the next level of the school system? It is important for us to consider what happens when our students reach the end of their schooling.

As I said, I was amazed that teachers were not equipping the students who arrived in my classroom with real-world thinking skills, but I never thought that I was part of the problem. After all, I came into education to make a difference. I worked hard to make my lessons engaging, and I was convinced my teaching was interesting and effective. Then along came Lisa.

Lisa was a lot like I had been. Having grown up with technology, she was completely comfortable using it. More important, she knew that technology would play a major role in her life, and she was determined to develop the technology skills she would need. She was an excellent student who consistently scored more than 90% on all her assignments and tests. I pegged her as a person destined for success. One day I asked Lisa a question—not a very unusual occurrence in a classroom, but for some reason what took place on this particular day absolutely rocked my world. The question I asked Lisa, which covered a major topic in the course, was the exact same question that I had asked on a test she had taken just two weeks earlier. She had answered the question correctly on the test, but, to my utter amazement, Lisa could not now answer the question in class. She knew we had covered the material, but she could not recall the specific answer. This stopped me in my tracks. Her inability to answer this question triggered a startling line of thought in my head. Just what exactly were students learning in my classes, anyway? If Lisa couldn't remember what we had covered recently, what about the other students who were not as academically capable? If students were so quickly forgetting the material I was presenting in my classes, then what were they left with? Was it possible that I was doing to Lisa and the other students exactly what had been done to me? Would they pass my course and then go on to encounter difficulty in the world outside school?

It dawned on me that I was mistaken in thinking that I was imparting truly useful knowledge to my students that they would be able to use later in life. Instead, I was teaching them how to cram for and write a test. But how often is a person's success at work dependent on the ability to write an exam? Although most employee evaluations are performance based, we don't use that type of evaluation very much in the school system. Much to my dismay, I realized that even with the best of intentions, there was something fundamentally wrong with my approach to teaching. I was producing "highly educated useless people." Instead of equipping students with useful real-world skills as I had hoped, what I was really doing in my classroom was teaching my students school skills.

SCHOOL SKILLS

School skills are those skills that are necessary for success inside the school system. They are very useful in school because they enable students to move to higher levels of schooling. School skills are focused on training students to perform well on written tests to get good grades. The central skill set involves cramming vast amounts of information into your mind for the purpose of low-level recall with the goal of getting higher test scores. A secondary set of skills focuses on retrieving details in the content of course material for the purpose of completing assignments. Hence, students in many classes are given worksheets to complete that require them to hunt for specific answers and fill in the blanks. This gives the teacher evidence that students have read the material for a course as well as prepares students for a test by providing them with sheets of details to study. In fact, many essay and report assignments are also little more than fill-in-the-blank exercises because the student is frequently given all of the criteria for such a project that outlines how the work should be done.

More often than not, assignments focus on the retrieving of the content rather than on the analysis of that information. In these exercises, teachers often give the message explicitly or implicitly that more is better—for example, by saying, "If you want an A on this assignment, then it must be at least five pages long." Consequently, the students develop research skills geared toward reporting as much content as possible, not on assessing that content for what it really means. We continue to focus almost exclusively on content right up to the time students leave us. Take a look at the curriculum in a Biology 12, English Literature 12, History 12, or Mathematics 12 class. The amount of material that must be covered is staggering. Most teachers do not turn their students loose on creative, high-level thinking projects because they can't afford the time such exercises take. Instead, they provide a lot of structure to keep students focused on absorbing course material. Although we aspire to teaching critical thought, our priority is really to cover the content in the curriculum, not to develop higher-level thinking skills. In our desire for our students to achieve higher test scores, we place too much emphasis on short-term memorization of content.

School skills are mainly concerned with the assimilation of content. They are based on the notion that information alone is all we need to give students to prepare them for life. The thinking goes that if a person comes to "know" a certain body of facts, they are educated and ready for the world at large. In his 1987 book, *Cultural Literacy*, E. D. Hirsch lists 15,000 facts he believes a person needs to know to be considered educated. His perspective on learning provides the rationale for many of the standards being set for education today. His facts provide the specific content that students must master. This powerful and pervasive view of education underlies much of what we are asked to do as teachers. A great deal of our time and effort goes into developing skills that empower our students to memorize facts.

School skills are not without value because they can earn students much positive feedback from teachers and parents. Eventually, if students master these skills well, these techniques can enable students to enter prestigious postsecondary institutions and to earn a considerable amount of money in scholarships. In addition, teachers and administrators receive accolades when their students demonstrate abilities with school skills. In some cases, school and district funding as well as promotions for administrators are tied to how well students acquire school skills.

School skills are very powerful, indeed! The entire education system is built around the teaching and testing of school skills. In light of all the emphasis that has been placed on developing school skills, it is critical that we ask a fundamental question: Are school skills the kind of skills that students will need to be successful when they leave the school system?

REAL-WORLD SKILLS

Some of you may be thinking, "Hold on, what's the big deal? Students have been graduating from our schools for years, and they have been able to do just fine in the working world. How can you now say that there's a problem with the way we are teaching students in school?" First of all, from my own personal experience at the map-making company I can tell you that, for some time, students have not been doing "just fine" in the working world after graduation. Furthermore, because the working world has changed radically in the last twenty-five years, there is an increased need for educators to prepare students differently for success in life in the 21st century.

In the last quarter century, the working world has undergone a significant change as a result of the explosion of microelectronics into everyday life. The power of this new technology to increase productivity and to reduce costs has been so compelling it has been implemented widely and quickly in the business world. This rapid proliferation of the use of electronic technology has upset the status quo that existed in the very stable late Industrial Age life of the 20th century. Not only has this technology changed the tools that people use in their jobs, it has forced businesses to reexamine the very premise of the Industrial Age—the compartmentalized, assembly-line thinking that breaks tasks into subtasks and requires people to become specialists in one small part of a much larger process.

In the Industrial Age workplace, most workers were not required to do much thinking at all—they simply learned the particular procedures for their part of the business or manufacturing task. Only the managers responsible for the whole process were required to think beyond a specific subtask. This organizational structure was the same whether you worked in a bank or on the production floor of an automobile company. In this environment, students could easily graduate from high school and fit right into most jobs without having independent problem-solving skills.

But this is not the case in a rapidly growing number of businesses today. There is an increasing demand for independent thought and high-level problem-solving ability from workers at all levels in the modern workplace. This demand has significant implications for education. Industrial Age schooling focused on rote memorization of content because these skills transferred well to the workplace, where Industrial Age businesses required the vast majority of their workers to memorize procedures for their jobs. In contrast, 21st century businesses have reorganized the way tasks get done. Such companies need workers who can use their minds for much more than just memorizing information; they need employees who can evaluate the relative importance of information and make judgments based on that evaluation, and workers who can creatively apply the power of new technology to increase productivity. They need people who can solve problems without direction from management. Here are two examples— one blue collar, one white collar—from the modern workplace.

Genie Industries in Redmond, Washington, is a company that typifies the new thinking in modern business. Genie is one of the world's largest producers of hydraulic lift equipment. Like many companies dealing with the changes in the global economy, Genie reorganized its operations twelve years ago to make the company more competitive. What is interesting about this reorganization is the empowerment of front-line workers to make decisions. As a result, the kind of thinking done by these workers has undergone a significant shift. Previously on the assembly line, each worker had a single specific job to do. All a worker had to worry about was his or her specific part of the assembly process. Management oversaw the efficiency of the production line as a whole and dealt with any problems that arose.

However, in the reorganized company, front-line workers are responsible for the entire production line. In the manufacturing of scissors lifts, for example, there is a series of red lights along the production line. One of these lights begins to flash when there is a problem holding up the assembly of lifts. When this occurs, workers on the line go to the trouble spot and solve the problem as quickly as possible. There is no abstract theory here; practical solutions are needed immediately so production can resume. The fact that bonuses are paid for keeping the assembly line moving provides real motivation for the front-line workers to be able to problem-solve effectively.

Another change in responsibility for front-line workers at Genie is a result of the company's "Rapid Improvement Program." The goal of this program is to continually improve the efficiency of the company's production process. In this program, workers who represent a wide cross-section of employees are pulled away from their jobs for a morning to tackle a problem of inefficiency in the manufacturing process. Ideas developed in the morning are implemented in the afternoon. Effective participation requires workers to use much higher-level thinking than was required before the company reorganized. Like workers at many new companies, workers at Genie are required to have problem-solving skills, teamwork skills, and effective communication skills. This new skill set is needed in addition to the basic technology skills—such as welding, painting, assembling, and so on—that have been required for the past thirty years. Blue-collar work simply isn't what it used to be.

White-collar work is also changing. Consider the kinds of skills required of employees who work in offices that are connected to the Internet. Many companies with branch offices in different time zones have realized that they can speed up production by forming multioffice work groups that work on projects longer than a standard eight-hour work day. The idea is that one branch office works on a project for an eight-hour shift and then passes the work along to another branch office in another time zone. That branch office works on the project for a shift and then passes the work on to another branch office in yet another time zone. International companies that use this strategy can work on projects twenty-four hours a day. Because much office work today is accomplished with computers that are connected to the Internet, the passing of work around the globe is actually quite straightforward. However, although connecting the computers is easy, getting workers to problem-solve jointly with people they never meet with face to face is a challenge. Success depends on creative thinking and effective communication by those involved. Workers have to think much farther ahead and anticipate problems. In addition, workers must be flexible because they must be able to respond to whatever problems or breakthroughs occurred while others were working on the project.

Now comes the critical question: Will traditional school skills used for writing tests and doing assignments prepare students for these kinds of working environments? The answer, of course, is no. Outside the school system, school skills won't cut it. For an increasing number of jobs in the modern workplace, completing worksheets, collecting information to write a report, or studying for multiple-choice tests does not equip students with the skills necessary for succeeding. Because the school system is so disconnected from the realities of the working world, it is quite possible for students to develop a skill set that works well inside, but not outside, school. Although school skills may help students get a scholarship or be admitted to a postsecondary institution, such skills probably won't be of much help when these former students get a job. If you consider how many university graduates are moving back home or going on to further study because they can't get a job, you begin to see the scope of the problem.

Furthermore, it is important to equip students with useful problem-solving skills because being able to think logically and independently is just as critical for solving personal and household problems as it is for solving work-related problems. What we are really talking about here is providing students with life skills. It is time for educators to reconsider the relevancy of what we teach.

"STAND AND DELIVER" LECTURE-STYLE TEACHING

We aspire to do good things for our students, to prepare them for success in the modern workplace. The reality, however, is that our teaching reinforces school skills much more than real-world skills. With the increased testing being brought into K–12 education in the last ten years, there is an overemphasis on the memorization of content. Let's listen in on a lesson being given in a Social Studies class, which is typical of the kind of teaching that takes place every day in thousands of classrooms across North America. What kind of skills are being developed, and what kind of thinking is being encouraged?

Students shuffle into the classroom, talking and playing around until the bell rings. The teacher gets up from the desk and starts speaking.

"OK, the bell has gone, so take out your notebooks and let's get started. Phillip, sit down and be quiet."

Just then, two students burst into laughter in the corner.

"Susan and Melissa, please get your books out and pay attention, or I'll have to separate you," says the teacher. "Julie, can you tell me what we were talking about at the end of the last class?"

After a short pause, Julie replies, "I can't remember . . . wasn't it something about Tokyo?"

"No, that's not correct," says the teacher. "If you would just learn to take better notes, you would do much better in this course. In fact, you all need to make sure you are taking better notes because next Tuesday morning there's going to be a . . ."

"Test," says the class collectively.

"That's right," replies the teacher, "so pay attention. We were talking about the Kansai region of Japan at the end of last class. The region has three major cities—Osaka, Kobe, and Kyoto. Now it is important that you remember the following information for your test. Osaka is the largest and most important city in this area. It is a major port and financial banking center, and the city functions as a hub for the region. It has a population of 2,506,000. The chief economic activity here is heavy manufacturing. Kobe is the next city we need to look at in the Kansai region. Kobe has a population of 1,459,000. It is also a port and, consequently, there is a large ship-building industry here. Kobe is also known for its steel smelters and textile production. Another point about Kobe is . . ."

The teacher looks up and realizes one of the students has not written down a single thing this period. He doesn't even have his notebook open.

"Bob, have you been sitting there this entire time without taking any notes at all?" the teacher asks incredulously.

"I don't have a pen," mumbles Bob, smiling nervously as he looks around at the other students.

"Well, borrow one!" bellows the teacher. The class waits while Bob gets a pen from one of the other students. Just as the teacher is about to begin teaching again, he notices one of the students passing a note to another.

"Barbara, give me that note." Barbara sheepishly hands the teacher the note and sits down.

"Now, where were we? Yes, the next major city in the Kansai region is Kyoto. Kyoto has a population of 1,461,000. The major economic activity here is heavy manufacturing, copper smelting, and chemical production."

"Hey, why do we have to learn this stuff, anyway?" interrupts one of the students.

"Because the Department of Education says so," replies the teacher. "It's the next section in the course outline. Now don't get off track, we still have some material to cover that you'll need for the test. We were talking about Kyoto. One of the most interesting aspects of this city is its history. In fact, Kyoto is so rich in cultural artifacts and historical sites that the Allies made a conscious decision to spare Kyoto from bombing during World War II. A unique feature of the transportation system in this area is the high-speed bullet train that links the three main cities.

"Now in preparation for the test next week, I want each of you to do a report on this region of Japan using pages 57 through 69 in your textbook. The report must list the population of each of the three cities, the major economic activity in each, and any special features. Please include a map and indicate the major transportation routes. You will get bonus marks if the map is colored."

What does the teacher focus on in this lesson? Does he concentrate on the process of solving problems? Is he intent on equipping students with skills that will serve them well in the long run when they leave the school system? No, the teacher in this lesson is focused on two short-term tasks: delivering the course content and classroom management. The goal is to cover the material in the curriculum so the students can write a test. The assignment reinforces the material to be memorized. The teacher is using the "stand and deliver" approach to instruction. Because the instruction is so boring, classroom management skills are required to keep the students on task. It is amazing how many teachers teach their classes this way.

Consider the role of the students in the Social Studies lesson we just heard. Are they active participants or passive listeners? What level of thinking is required to function successfully while in class and while doing the homework report? What level of thought will be required to do well on the test? The truth is that students will need little more than low-level recall skills to be successful in this class. But that leads us to a critical question: What practical skill development has taken place here that will be useful for these students in the long term? Is coloring a map an important real-world skill? Is memorizing the specific information about this region of Japan going to yield a valuable skill for students after they graduate? When the students forget most of the specific content (as we know they will in the long run), what will they be left with? They will be left with school skills, the kind of skills I had when I ventured out of the school system and promptly got fired. These students will be able to take notes on the most important facts in a presentation from a teacher, read a textbook, and do a report that reinforces those facts. Then, they will be able to recall that material for a written test a few days later. The problem is that these skills are not widely in use in the world outside school.

THE MYTH OF POSTSECONDARY EDUCATION

Many teachers argue that the skills students currently acquire in public school are necessary and valuable for their success in postsecondary schooling. These teachers consider it their primary job to prepare students for schooling after high school graduation. They claim that they don't have to focus on practical skills because students will get their real-world training when they go to a postsecondary institution. However, the fact is that most students in high school do not attend, let alone graduate from, universities or other postsecondary institutions. Barry Schuller, the president of AOL Time Warner, said that his research indicated that only 21% of adults have a university degree by the time they reach the age of 30 (Schuller, 2000). According to *USA*

Today, the U.S. Census Bureau's Educational Attainment in the United States 2003 Study says only 27.2% of high school graduates 25 and older had at least a bachelor's degree ("More People," 2004). It is clear that the majority of students graduating from high school will not graduate from college. But if you walk into any high school, you will find that the overwhelming majority of courses and counseling are focused on getting students ready for postsecondary education. The educational system is clearly out of sync with the realities of the world outside. By ignoring where students actually go after they graduate from school, we are not equipping them with the skills they need for success in the world they will face upon graduation.

It is critical that teachers, administrators, bureaucrats, politicians, and parents understand the myth of postsecondary education. Higher education is simply not in the future of most young people. And of those who actually attend a postsecondary institution, many will not graduate. Furthermore, of those who do graduate, only those in specialized programs will have acquired skills that will help them get a job. That brings us to another very important question for educators teaching in the K–12 school system: Where do the majority of students get the skills necessary for success in the world of work? The answer is that most people must survive in the working world with the skills they learn in their K–12 schooling. But if students don't possess relevant job-ready skills when they leave Grade 12, how are they going to get good jobs, if they can get jobs at all?

IT'S TIME TO RETHINK HOW WE TEACH

Some of you may be thinking that it is all well and good to talk about the irrelevancy of teaching methods that result in students learning only school skills; however, with the massive amount of material in the curriculum to be covered and with the increased testing students face, teachers have little choice but to focus on content delivery in their classrooms. Besides, there are a lot of people who equate knowing facts with being educated. So it looks like focusing on teaching content to students is here to stay.

Of course students must learn content in school. I agree with Mr. Hirsch that to be educated, students must know a certain body of information about the world around them. Certainly, an educated person should have an appreciation of history, art, music, geography, languages, government, literature, science, and mathematics. However, an educated person must also have the ability to think logically and to solve problems effectively. Learning specific facts without acquiring the thinking skills necessary to assess the significance of those facts is of little lasting value. If the focus of our teaching remains on content, our students will develop only school skills. But students will need more than school skills to be successful when their schooling is over. Students need reasoning skills if they are going to be successful in the world of the 21st century. And they need to acquire these skills in their K–12 education because the majority of students will not go on to complete a postsecondary program.

It is clear that we need to rethink how we teach students if we want to prepare them for the world they will encounter when they leave the school system. In the technologically saturated world of the 21st century, it would be easy to assume that the answer is to simply equip students with up-to-date technology skills. Technology skills are important, but they are not enough. What is needed is a fundamental shift in the way we present material to students. We need an instructional approach that will equip students with real-world, problem-solving skills plus teach them the content they must master to be an educated person. As presented in Chapters 2 and 3, this requires educators to question some long-held ideas about what teaching should look like.

CHAPTER TWO

Six Ways to Teach for Independent and Higher Learning

My goal when I started teaching was to equip my students with problem-solving skills that would allow them to function in the world outside school. Not knowing any other approach, I began my career by teaching the same way I had been taught—I presented material to students and then gave them assignments to complete. When we finished a unit or reached the end of a term, I gave the students a test. This approach, modeled for me in all my years as a student, was reinforced by my professors when I entered teacher training. Using this method was as natural as breathing. However, this approach did not prove to be satisfactory. Students continually relied on me for just about everything that happened in the classroom. They waited for me to tell them what the assignments were. They wanted assurance from me that the answers they were getting were the right ones. They stopped working when they ran into problems and seemed paralyzed until I gave them direction. They were so focused on grades that they thwarted my efforts to get them to consider ideas and attitudes of mind that were not specifically on my tests. I thought if I could just motivate them somehow, they would embrace higher-level learning. Over the years, I became increasingly frustrated in my attempts to develop real-world, independent thinking skills in my students. The harder I tried, the more frustrated I became. Why couldn't I wean students of their dependence on me?

It took me years to realize that I, not the students, was the problem. My method of instruction and evaluation was actually fostering the dependence in students that I found so troubling. Not only was my focus on memorization of content yielding low-level thinking skills, it was boring my students to tears. I eventually realized that to be effective, I had to get beyond most of the teaching that had been modeled to me as a student and as a student teacher. I needed to get rid of those aspects of my teaching that were counterproductive to developing independent, higher-level thinking in my students. I needed to get outside the box of what I thought teaching should look like and embrace new ways of presenting tasks to students that both covered the material in my curriculum guide as well as taught students how to analyze the material to solve problems.

The teaching method I outline in this chapter comes from my twenty-four years of experience in the classroom trying to formulate an instructional method to cultivate independent, higher-level thinking in my students in a way that captures their interest. The approach I developed is based on six significant changes to the way we present tasks to students and evaluate their work.

RESISTING THE TEMPTATION TO "TELL"

Six Ways to Teach for Independent and Higher Learning

1. We must resist the temptation to "tell."

I remember watching my own children go through the school system. Their time in kindergarten was a wonderful mix of discovery experiences. Their teacher was masterful at making learning fun and exciting. It was a joy watching them learn how to read and write in the midst of all the fun. I wanted to be a student in that classroom! As my children progressed through elementary school, they began to do more serious work in terms of reports and tests. Instead of enjoying discovery learning experiences, they were increasingly told what they needed to know by their teachers. By the time they reached junior high school, learning was no longer fun; it was serious business, and their role was to sit and listen to their teachers tell them what they needed to know. Both of my kids complained that subjects in junior high school were no longer very interesting. How could these teachers rob my kids of their desire to learn by talking at them?

Although I was critical of my children's teachers, it never occurred to me that I was doing the same thing to the students in my classes. (That's the amazing thing about human nature—it is so easy to see what others are doing wrong, but so hard to see it in yourself.) However, the longer I taught, the more I came to recognize that the desire to tell students things was also deeply embedded in the way I approached teaching. Even though I had great visions of high-level thinking activities taking place in my classes, the reality was that when the door closed and I was left all alone with thirty students staring at me, I stood up in front of the class and told them everything I thought they needed to know.

As discussed in Chapter 1, this "stand and deliver" approach to instruction is widely used by teachers. We do research on some aspect of our curriculum, and then we can't wait to get to class to tell our students what we have discovered. We prepare handouts that tell students what they need to know for the next test. Sometimes the desire to tell is so strong that we even read to students from the textbook when they could easily read it for themselves.

Consider the impact this kind of teaching has on students. Because "telling" is the typical instructional style in many classrooms, students endure this kind of experience in subject after subject. Consequently, students look for something—anything—to distract them from the tedium of listening to someone telling them seemingly irrelevant information. Teachers can end up spending a great deal of time on classroom management because it is so hard for young people to sit through this kind of experience day after day.

Where does this desire to "tell" come from? By the time a person returns to school as a teacher, the telling method of instruction has been modeled over and over from elementary school through university. For some people, telling is the only method of instruction they have ever experienced. It's no wonder that telling is teachers' native language. For some, telling comes from the need to be seen as an expert. For others, it is simply the quickest and easiest way to get through a lot of material. I know for myself that when push comes to shove and I have to get through some material quickly in one of my courses, I close my classroom door and begin telling students what they need to know. Whatever the reason, telling has a powerful hold on the teaching profession. We persist in using it as the prime method of instruction even though there are strong indications that telling is the least effective way for students to learn.

Why is telling such an inadequate way to teach? Because it takes the excitement of discovery out of learning. Life is an adventure, and finding out how the world works should be a wonderfully interesting endeavor. Telling deprives learners of the firsthand experience of finding out for themselves. Think about what it is like seeing a suspense movie without knowing anything about the plot. Watching the characters narrowly escape certain death while the music creates a suspenseful atmosphere gets your heart pumping as you sit on the edge of your seat waiting to see if they make it through the ordeal safely. Now consider how different your experience would be if, before you saw the movie, someone told you the whole story. Would you sit on the edge of your seat waiting to see what would happen next? No. Knowing the ending would ruin the suspense that keeps you intensely engaged in the movie's progress. When it comes to learning, telling does the same thing—it removes the suspense that keeps a student engaged in new material. Telling takes the fun of discovery out of learning.

Why is discovery so important? Because it generates interest in learning, and interest is critical to learning. In his book *Information Anxiety 2*, Richard Saul Wurman captured the essential role of interest in learning when he wrote the following:

> Learning can be seen as the acquisition of information. But before it can take place, there must be interest. Interest permeates all endeavors and precedes learning. In order to acquire and remember new knowledge, it must stimulate your curiosity in some way. (Wurman, 2001, p. 85)

Wurman goes on to say that giving students content without generating any interest in the material is like having only one side of a piece of Velcro—it just doesn't stick. I like that analogy. I believe the chief role we have as teachers is to generate interest in the material we must teach. It is our job to create the other side of the Velcro so the learning sticks in the minds of our students. This is no easy task because some of the material we must cover is dry, and learning it can be tedious. Making all of a course's content interesting can tax a teacher's expertise and ingenuity to the maximum. However, like parents who have to figure out a way for their child to take some unpleasant medicine, a teacher must use creativity and imagination to generate the interest needed to make instruction more palatable for their students.

Telling also removes the motivation for students to learn on their own. There is no need for students to take the initiative to pursue a subject when they know someone else is going to tell them what they need to know. This is a key point when we consider how to prepare students for the working world of the 21st century. When students leave the school system to become entrepreneurs and knowledge workers, they will need to be internally motivated because no one will be telling them everything they need to know. They will need to determine not only what knowledge and skills are required to accomplish each task, but they also must then search out that information and acquire those skills on their own.

Telling will always have a place in a teacher's instructional repertoire, especially when they must deliver a lot of content in a short period of time. However, to counterbalance the telling that students will receive, we need to shift our instruction to include discovery learning. According to noted psychologist Carl Rogers in his 1994 book, *Freedom to Learn,* self-discovered learning is the only learning that significantly influences a person's behavior. We must remember that telling someone something, even if we are keenly interested in what we have to tell, removes the firsthand experience of discovery from the person we tell. From politics to history to physics to biology, finding out why things are the way they are and what makes them tick can be a wonderful journey of discovery for a young mind. The material may be as old as the hills and well known to the teacher, but if a young person discovers something for the first time, it is a new experience that brings interest and excitement to the learning endeavor.

PROVIDING CONTEXT TO CONTENT

Six Ways to Teach for
Independent and Higher Learning

1. We must resist the temptation to "tell."

2. We must stop teaching decontextualized content.

Early in my teaching career, I encountered a disconcerting apathy in my students toward many of the topics that had to be learned in my classes. Students would often remark, "Why do I have to learn this stuff?" I was unprepared for this question. Often teachers aren't sure why students have to learn something, either. Explaining to students that this material is the next section in the curriculum guide isn't exactly persuasive.

I am convinced that students develop an attitude of apathy toward their schoolwork because they do not see how it is relevant to their daily lives. Certainly, some of the material students must digest to become educated is not immediately applicable to what they are going to do that afternoon. However, there appears to be a prevalent attitude among teachers that it is not necessary to relate what they teach in school to life in general. Perhaps establishing a connection between schoolwork and the real world is a challenge for teachers because many of them have spent little time in jobs outside the school system and thus do not have a broad base of working-world experience to draw upon.

Whatever the reason, many teachers do not relate learning in the classroom to real-world situations. We are experts at giving theory without providing a practical context. We can cover a curriculum and test the recall of the material, but we often don't equip students with anything more than the ability to regurgitate meaningless facts. We carry the big stick of the test, which forces students to work their way through the material to be covered, but such student learning is, for the most part, incredibly low level.

My colleague Ian Jukes uses the following illustration to demonstrate the power of context for enhancing learning. For those of you who are old enough to remember when a man first stood on the moon, can you recall where you were and what you were doing when it happened? For those of you who are younger, think of a major political, international, or sports event, such as the September 11th terrorist attacks, the fall of the Berlin Wall, or the upset of the St. Louis Rams by the New England Patriots in the 2002 Super Bowl. Or remember a significant event in your personal life, like when you proposed marriage, when you learned of the death of a family member, or when your child took his or her first steps. Most of you will find that not only can you remember the specific event, but you can also remember the circumstances of where you were and what you were doing when it happened. Why can you remember the specifics of what you were doing that day when you have forgotten so many others? The reason is that the context of the significant event provides a frame of reference that enables you to remember specific information about what you were doing at that moment long after the event took place.

The power of context also plays an important role in learning. Placing course content in the context of a real-world scenario helps a student remember specific details of a lesson because the context gives the information meaning. The real-world context allows the student to connect the new data with what he or she has already learned about life. Without this connection, new information is not meaningful and is therefore not stored in the student's brain for long-term recall. In his 2001 book, *How the Brain Learns,* David Sousa states that when the brain receives new information, it places the data in working memory or short-term memory. This memory lasts for only 18 to 24 hours before it is lost unless a connection is made between the new material and the content in a person's long-term memory. Creating meaning by placing course content in a real-world context is a key factor in long-term memory. To be stored in long-term memory, new information must meet two key criteria. Sousa states these criteria in the form of two questions: Does this new information make sense? Does it have meaning? Most teachers focus on creating lessons and assignments that make sense so that students can understand them. This, however, is only half of what is needed. As Sousa goes on to say,

> Teachers spend 90 percent of their planning time devising lessons so that students will understand the learning objective. But to convince a learner's brain to persist with that objective, teachers need to be more mindful of helping students establish meaning. (Sousa, 2001, p. 49)

If meaning is absent from the presentation of new material, students don't store it for very long. Placing new information in the context of a real-world scenario provides the frame of reference the mind needs to retain that content. Thus, creating a meaningful context for new learning is a critical factor in developing long-term adhesion of new information to a student's memory.

This idea holds great promise for educators when they are attempting to get students to remember course content. By providing a real-world context for new information, teachers are actually helping students develop memory connections that facilitate long-term information recall. This strategy would have helped me teach my student Lisa, who couldn't remember course content I had taught her only two weeks earlier. If I had created a meaningful real-world context for the material I had taught her, she would not only have had a much better chance of remembering the material for the test, but, more important, she would have had a much better chance of remembering the information years later. This power of context to assist with learning is worthy of note for those teachers who are struggling with preparing students for large standardized tests. By providing a context for the information, teachers are actually helping students learn the material so their recall will be better when they write the test. In addition and more important, a meaningful real-world context helps students remember over the long term.

If students aren't asked to apply their learning to actual situations, they do not develop the skill of transferring school learning to life. We simply must begin to make a real-world link in our teaching. This will have two major benefits. First, students will begin to develop real-world thinking skills because they are tackling the kinds of tasks they will encounter when they leave school. Second, students will find the task of learning more interesting because they can see that the tasks they work on in school have more relevance to their life, even if it will be a few years before the knowledge and skills acquired in school are fully utilized. A real-world context for learning is a key way to engage students in learning.

Consider the skills students have developed when they have been taught without being given a real context for their learning. Are those skills really that useful in the working world? Dave Master (1999), a former teacher and now the director of artist development and training at Warner Brothers, asks educators to consider which of the following people they would hire if they owned a construction business:

A. A person who could identify a hammer.

B. A person who could define a hammer.

C. A person who could write a composition about a hammer.

D. A person who could use a computer simulation of a hammer.

E. A person who could use a hammer to drive a nail in a lab.

F. A person who could build a small structure using a hammer in concert with other tools.

The answer is obvious. The person who could apply hammering skills to do something useful, like build a small structure, is clearly the only person on the list you would want to hire. Notice that the first five people had school skills only. They may have adequate abilities to move ahead in the school system, but they don't have much skill that will help them in a construction job when they leave. Only the person in option F displays the kinds of skills that are useful in the workplace. Master concludes his exercise by asking, if you wouldn't hire someone who had only any of the first five school skills without the practical use of those skills, why should you expect employers to hire your students if all they have are school skills without any practice applying those skills to real-life situations?

The only way we are going to equip our students with really useful skills is to provide a real-world context for the learning that takes place in the classroom. Furthermore, this real-world context learning must not be limited to the elective courses in computing, business, and shop; it must occur across the curriculum. English courses, for example, could be taught in the context of students acting as employees at a publishing company. They would still learn about William Shakespeare or George Orwell, but their assignments could also relate to the publishing of a magazine. Critical analysis of the plot development or foreshadowing in George Orwell's *1984* could take the form of editorials or articles for the magazine. At the same time, dealing with the tasks and deadlines for producing the magazine would give students experience with the reality of working in the publishing business.

Similarly, science classes could be taught with the students acting as workers at an environmental protection agency. Students in a history class could be military strategists. A geography class could be a map publishing company. Math students could be working for a public opinion polling company. The possibilities are endless; all it takes is imagination on the part of the teacher and some research into the kind of business activities a particular kind of company would do. This creativity on the part of teachers pays real dividends with students, who will emerge from the classroom both better prepared for the larger world outside the school system and much more likely to remember specific information for a longer period of time.

FOSTERING INDEPENDENT THINKING

Six Ways to Teach for
Independent and Higher Learning

1. We must resist the temptation to "tell."

2. We must stop teaching decontextualized content.

3. We must stop giving students the final product of our thinking.

When I taught Mathematics in my first year as a teacher, one day I had to do a proof of a mathematical concept on the board for my students. I was feeling very good about myself as I explained each step of the proof, certain that the students were impressed with my mathematical prowess. Then the wheels fell off the cart! I reached the end of the proof and it did not work out. I quickly erased the board and began again. It didn't work out the second time either. I tried again—same thing. I felt humiliated. Most teachers have had similar experiences at one time or another in their careers. What do you think I did about this situation? I went home and I worked on that proof over and over again until I could do it forward and backward without a hitch.

The next time I saw my Mathematics class, I did the proof flawlessly. I can distinctly remember a student looking at what I had done and remarking, "I could never do that." I remember my confidence being bolstered by his comment, taking it as confirmation that I had recovered totally from my blunder in the previous class and that the students' faith in my mathematical skills had been restored. Unfortunately, it was years later before I realized the profound truth in what my young Math student had said. He was completely correct in saying he could never do what I had done. What I failed to recognize at the time was that it was the way I presented the material that made mastering that mathematics skill unreachable for him.

My teaching was ineffective because I had done all my thinking and learning behind closed doors. I showed my students only the final product of all my hard work. They never saw the sweat that went into acquiring the skill that I demonstrated the second time I did the proof for them. They never saw the multiple times I went through the proof. They never saw the trial-and-error approach I followed when I encountered difficulties. They didn't witness the messy nature of the raw thinking that takes place during the struggle we all endure when trying to learn new skills and solve problems. By simply showing the final result of my thinking instead of modeling the learning process, I made it difficult, if not impossible, for all but the mathematically gifted students in my class to be successful.

I believe that many teachers fall into the same trap I did of doing all the thinking for their students behind closed doors. When students are assigned a worksheet, who picked the topic for the exercise? Who decided what questions to ask? When we give students a report to do, who did all the work in thinking up the project? Who decided that one section would be worth more points than the other? Who determined the rationale for including some information and excluding other content? Who decided where the students would find the information? Of course, students need the scaffolding of some structure to the assignment and guidance from the teacher to help them do the work we give them, but is it possible that in the name of expediency teachers provide much more than they should if they want students to develop independent thinking skills?

If we hope to foster student independence, then it is important that teachers start giving more of the decision-making responsibility to their students. That means we must resist the temptation to do all the preliminary work for our students. We must place our priority on student learning over expediency for the teacher.

MOVING TO PROBLEM SOLVING

Six Ways to Teach for Independent and Higher Learning

1. We must resist the temptation to "tell."

2. We must stop teaching decontextualized content.

3. We must stop giving students the final product of our thinking.

4. **We must make a fundamental shift—problems first, teaching second.**

Why are students not engaged by the tasks we give them in school? Why do we have to threaten, cajole, and plead to inspire them to do the work we give them every day? Is it possible the way we present schoolwork to students is the cause of their resistance? Consider how the tasks in school are given to students. Students begin their work in a Science class with the teacher saying, "All right, class, today we will be looking at the water cycle." After a brief discussion on where rain comes from, the teacher finishes the lesson by saying, "I want you to read pages 23 though 26 in your textbook and answer all twelve questions on page 27." Does this approach really foster discovery learning? Does it provide the answer to a question the students have about the world around them? Does it lay out some problem that the students must solve? Does it develop anything beyond school skills in the students?

Think about the way tasks and problems are presented daily in our personal and professional lives. Does someone outline all of the parameters and specifications for us? Does someone do the initial research for where the resources are located for solving this problem? Does someone break down the task into more easily handled subsections? Of course not, yet that is exactly what teachers do for students every day. And I don't mean just for the younger ones—I have seen assignments given to senior high school students where all the groundwork was laid out for them on the assignment sheet, and the only thing left for the students to do was fill in the blanks. Assigning students tasks where the groundwork has already been done by the teacher is like giving students the answer before giving them the question. More than half the work of developing the solution to a problem is already done by the teacher before the students are involved. The teacher has decided the order of the questions, the priority of points in the material, and the information to be ignored. In short, the teacher has done all of the work of defining the problem and has laid it out on a piece of paper.

However, real-world problems do not come with the task neatly outlined on a sheet of paper. In the workplace, they are contained in conversations with our boss, coworkers, clients, and so on. They are revealed as we are following the steps of some manufacturing process. They dawn on us as we encounter inefficiencies in the way goods are moved or people are handled. Problems are presented to us when talking to our clients, who have real needs as they go about their daily business. Problems in your personal life are discovered as you talk about your plans or feelings with your family and friends. Real-world problems are revealed in roundabout ways. They do not arrive already thought out and neatly packaged. It dawned on me that I needed to present problems to my students in the same way—as incomplete statements of tasks to be done, where the students must do some detective work to discover the true nature of the problem. It is critical that we begin to model the way problems and tasks are presented in the world outside school if we want students to develop the skills necessary for survival in a world without worksheets and project outlines.

I have observed that something wonderful happens when you give young people a real-world problem to solve. It's like dumping out the pieces of a jigsaw puzzle on a table; the unfinished nature of the puzzle appeals to the mind to figure out a solution. Problems engage the mind, teasing and tempting the brain to find a solution. Giving students a problem to solve presents them with an unfinished picture that begs to be completed and that draws them into the task.

To challenge my students to see problem solving as detective work, I use role playing extensively in my classes as a way to present new tasks. There are several benefits to this approach. First, by taking on the role of a person from the business world or local community, students begin to get the perspective of people from outside the school system. Although my experience in business has certainly helped me create realistic scenarios for my classes, I don't have the necessary expertise to make a convincing role play for all of the problems I want students to solve. I have discovered a great resource for creating realistic role plays lies in parents and former students who are service advisors, engineers, computer salespeople, restaurant managers, and so on. When I invite them to the classroom, they bring different perspectives to problems and add genuine touches of realism that I couldn't provide on my own. Role playing provides a great way to make a real-world link to classroom tasks.

A second benefit of the role-play approach is that when I am in a role play, students do not have access to my expertise as a teacher. For example, if I am acting as the owner of a local auto parts business in need of a computer network, the students cannot ask me anything about how to design a network because, in the role of auto parts store owner, I know a lot about car parts but not very much about computers. Because they must think their way through solving this problem on their own without access to my knowledge on the topic, students begin to develop independent thinking skills.

Indeed, when the teacher takes on a real-life position from outside the classroom to present a task, students naturally shift into real-world roles for themselves when they solve the problem. For example, let's say a teacher walks into the classroom and introduces herself as the manager of a biomedical laboratory. The lab is having a problem with bacterial outbreaks occurring when certain tests are done on urine, and she says she needs the students to find a way to stop the bacteria from growing. Instinctively, the students take on the role of laboratory consultants as they apply their knowledge of biology and chemistry to solve this problem. Not only are the students covering the material in the curriculum guide, this real-life simulation gives them practice at doing various kinds of jobs.

The Shift From Telling to Discovery

Let's return to the Social Studies lesson on the Kansai Region that we presented in Chapter 1. Is it possible to use a role play to present this task to students so they take on a real-world role while at the same time learning about the geography, culture, and economy of this part of the world? Consider the impact of the following presentation to the same Social Studies class.

Students shuffle into the classroom, talking and playing around until the bell rings. The teacher gets up from the desk and starts speaking.

"Today I want you to be travel agents. Now, there are a lot of travel agents in this community, so I want you to remember our class discussions about the concept of 'value-added.' You will recall that when you are offering goods or services that are similar to those offered by other companies, the only way to compete effectively is to add value that others don't offer. In addition to the normal services of a travel agent, the value I want you to add in this situation is an informational service that provides your customers with relevant material that will make their business or pleasure trips more effective and enjoyable. You are about to get a call from Trans Pacific Shipping, one of your largest corporate customers.

"Good morning, it's Tim Johnson at Trans Pacific calling. Our company is considering sending three executives to the Kansai Region of Japan two weeks from tomorrow. The plan calls for them to spend two nights in the city of Osaka, two nights in the city of Kobe, and two nights in the city of Kyoto. We'll need costs for travel and accommodations, and of course we'll expect you to make up an itinerary for the flights. Our executives will also need to know the best way to get around while they are there, so please include local transportation in the itinerary. The purpose of the trip is to explore the possibility of building a branch office in the Kansai area. We ship via containers on ocean freighters, so we will need you to recommend the city in which we should locate our new office based on port and financial services. Also, these executives have been working hard, so we want to build three days of rest and relaxation into the trip. Any suggestions for popular tourist-type activities would be most helpful; the employees happen to be very interested in 20th century history.

"We have to make a quick decision on whether to go ahead with this trip, so we will need a group of three of you to come and make a presentation to our board of directors next Tuesday. We'd also like you to leave some printed materials that we can examine after your presentation is over. Please keep track of your time and give us a bill for your services when you meet the board of directors. We are looking forward to seeing you next Tuesday."

Compare the effect of this instructional approach with that used by the Social Studies teacher on the same topic in Chapter 1. Will this task be more or less engaging than the first? Who is responsible for the learning when this task is given to a class of students? In the real-world simulation approach, will the students encounter all of the factual material that was presented in the lesson given by the Social Studies teacher using the telling approach in the previous chapter? For example, will the students discover the major economic activity in each of the three cities in this region of Japan? Will they find out that there is a high-speed bullet train connecting the cities? Will they unearth the fact that Kyoto was spared from Allied bombs during the Second World War? Yes, but with three significant differences in the way they learn the material. First, they will discover this material rather than being told this material. Second, the problem they are solving for Trans Pacific Shipping gives them a good reason for learning this information. Third, making a recommendation for the best location of the new branch office forces students to use higher-level thinking to compare the three cities using the criteria Mr. Johnson has outlined instead of simply regurgitating facts as they fill in the blanks.

One of the things I enjoy most about using the real-world simulation approach is observing the response I get from students when they are given their first task in this manner. They are nonplussed! Here is how I begin the year with my senior technology classes.

After I address all the "administrivia" associated with school start-up, I stand up and say to my class,

"Good morning, my name is Mr. Henderson, and I own a local commercial painting business. The reason I asked to meet with you this morning is that I need a Web site for my business that will promote our company to prospective clients. We would like the site to start with an animated introduction page. We want the menu of options to stay on the screen at all times, and we would like a rotating logo in the upper-left corner, if possible. Do you have any questions?"

Students usually just stare at me in silence. Then I sit down.

It is important to note that I do this before I have taught them any of the skills necessary to do this task. How do you suppose the students respond after I sit down? Amazingly, after a few more moments of silence, they begin to talk to each other about their summer, their plans for after school, and various other items of interest to 16- and 17-year-olds. They are waiting for me to tell them what to do. So, after a few minutes have passed, I stand up and say,

"I forgot to mention that this Web site project for Mr. Henderson is worth one hundred marks and it is due in one week."

Now what do you imagine the response is from the students? It ranges from incredulity to outright rage.

"You can't expect us to do this in one week—we don't know how to create Web animations or rotating logos!" someone will say.

"That is a statement. I don't know how to respond to that," I reply.

"Well, aren't you going to teach us anything?" a student will fire back.

"I will be happy to answer any specific questions you have that relate to the task Mr. Henderson has given you to do," is my response.

And so begins a dialogue concerning how to create the various parts of the Web site. The great thing about giving students tasks in the form of a problem is that problems lead to questions. Students learn to ask the right questions because I don't give them anything more than a rough outline of the problem to be solved. And those questions lead to ownership of the task by the students. And that ownership leads to independent thought, which is our goal.

Students soon learn the importance of being self-reliant because I decline to answer any of their questions. For example, when I return to my role as a classroom teacher after role playing Mr. Henderson, students will invariably ask me questions that only the role-play person can answer. I reply that because I wasn't at the meeting, I am not able to answer those questions. When students realize I won't bail them out in subsequent tasks, they begin to learn to analyze the task as soon as it is presented, to formulate significant questions, and to overcome their shyness about asking their questions to get the answers they need to accomplish the task successfully. An added bonus is that students learn to take full and complete notes of meetings with role-play personalities. I don't have to drone on and on about the need for doing this—experience is the best teacher.

When I present students with a new task, I usually ask them to act as a person in a real-world job. I have discovered that they love the chance to try out different roles from the working world. Young people are trying to figure out where they fit into this thing called life, and they eagerly take on the roles I ask of them. It's like "playing" real life. By providing them an opportunity to take on a role from the working world, students begin to think about the kinds of tasks people in those jobs do, which has led to some unexpected side benefits. I have been pleasantly surprised at parent/teacher interview night when parents will tell me that their son or daughter has been asking them questions about what they do at work because it relates to a role I have asked the students to assume.

Transforming Your Curriculum With Real-World Role Play

The real-world simulation/role-play approach just discussed can work with any material you need to cover in your classes. Just take an outcome or group of outcomes from your curriculum guide and create a problem for your students to solve. Here are the keys:

- The problem must address the outcomes in the curriculum guide. If the problem is solved with all of the specifications addressed, then the students will have covered the required material in the course.
- The problem should have a real-world link. The scenario doesn't have to be a business problem; it could have to do with someone's personal life, recreation, personal finances,

local or national politics, the environment, a pressing global issue like world hunger, and so on.

- You must ensure that you do not give the answer when presenting the problem.

The real-world simulation approach can be used in any subject. The following is an example of a problem that could be given in a science class when the teacher wants students to learn about the water cycle and the chemicals that can be picked up as water makes its way back to the ocean. The teacher knows that the students' textbook says that phenol chlorides are contained in many of the pesticides commonly used by farmers. Instead of telling the students that rainwater will pick up the pesticides farmers put on their fields, the teacher presents the students with the following problem to solve.

"Today, I want you to be scientists working for the Department of the Environment for the state/provincial government. Your boss walks into your office and tells you the following.

"I don't care what you are working on—drop it. I have something that has to be dealt with immediately. Last month we got a phone call from a man in Plainville in the farming area just north of Smalltown. He reported that fish had died in Bonson Creek after a heavy rainfall. Unfortunately, the message from that phone call got lost here in the office and we didn't respond to the man. Well, more fish died two days ago after another heavy rainfall, and the man has gone to the local media with the story. That makes us look pretty bad, so the pressure is on to find out what the problem is and what can be done to make sure that fish don't die again. I had Terry Johnson go out and start work on this yesterday, but she has called in sick this morning. So here is what we have. Terry had the water in the creek analyzed, and we have found high levels of phenol chlorides dissolved in the water. She also interviewed some of the farmers in the area, and here are her notes. I need to know what phenol chlorides are and where they came from."

The Role of Technology in Teaching for Tomorrow

At this point, you might be wondering why a book about preparing students for success in the 21st century has gone on so long without an in-depth discussion of the use of technology. The reason is that technology is simply a tool, albeit a powerful one, that helps us get jobs done. The mind that controls the technology is far more important than the technology itself. Therefore, this book focuses on how we can get students to develop high-level, problem-solving thinking skills. There is no doubt that technology is increasing in power and invading more of our daily lives. However, regardless of what technology students have at their disposal in the future, problem-solving skills will be the critical factor that determines their success.

The key to using technology effectively in the classroom lies in crafting reality simulation tasks for students that target the material in the curriculum to be covered in a course. For example, if an outcome in the curriculum is for students to demonstrate the ability to use a spreadsheet to create a bar graph, the teacher must specify that such a graph is required. When the problem is presented to students, the teacher could role-play a sales manager for a local car dealership who needs an office worker (the student) to perform a certain task—for example, to create a graphical representation of car sales by each salesperson or the inventory of cars showing each model—so the manager can make better business decisions for the dealership. Another example is the travel agent problem discussed earlier in this chapter. Consider how the specifications will require students to use technology to successfully complete that project. How else could they possibly find out the cost and schedule of flights to Japan, the schedule for the high-speed trains in the Kansai Region, the cost of hotels, and so on in time for the presentation to the board of directors if they didn't access that information on the Internet? Technology tools provide the best means for creating the presentation to the board of directors and for producing the printed materials that were requested. Creating specifications for a task that require students to use a word processor, a spreadsheet, the Internet, a digital camera, and so on is the key to getting students to use technological tools.

Here is another example of how technology can be incorporated across the curriculum. In an English class in which the teacher wants students to revise their written work using a word processor, students could role-play employees of a publishing company working on an upcoming issue of a magazine. Modern publishers make extensive use of electronic technology, so students would be expected to use electronic tools to accomplish the assigned task. Because this is an English class, the material being discussed in the magazine could be a novel and a short story that are specified in the curriculum for the course. Here is how the task could be presented to students.

"OK, let's get this staff meeting going," says the teacher, taking on the role of magazine editor. "We have a problem that must be dealt with this week. We have two articles scheduled to be published in the next issue of *Modern Literature* magazine due out in two weeks—an editorial piece on *Lord of the Flies* and a review of a new short story by Steven King. We contracted someone to write these two pieces and she was paid. Unfortunately, because we have been so busy around here, her work was never checked, and there are some major problems. First, both the pieces have a number of errors in grammar and spelling. Second, they are too long; we need both articles to fit on a single piece of paper. So we need you to work with another staff member to ensure this work gets edited correctly. The work was submitted as Microsoft Word files and can be accessed on our server in the To Be Completed directory; the file names are LOF Editorial and King Story Review. Each member of your team is responsible for one of the articles. We want each of you to print out the existing work and edit the hard copy using standard editing symbols. Enter those corrections into the computer and print out a copy of your edited version for your partner to edit. Edited files must be placed on the server by noon Friday. We want to see the original hard copy as well as both edited versions of each article in case we need to get more information when copyfitting. Any questions?"

The following is a more complex technology assignment that requires students to use content from two different subject areas (which occurs often in the real world). Students will need information from both their Social Studies and Science classes to complete this task. In addition to incorporating aspects of Social Studies and Science, this assignment provides students with the opportunity to learn how to use 21st century communication technology while working with a remote partner whom they don't meet face to face. Instead, they will meet in cyberspace and share their work electronically. The purpose of this electronic collaboration is to plan and create a Web site. Students in the Social Studies class are told they are working for "Go Green," a nonprofit environmental organization, as urban planners. They are told that their education has been in economic geography and that they are experts in land use planning. Students in the Science class are told they are working as biologists for the nonprofit environmental organization "Save The Planet." The Science students are told they are experts in understanding wildlife in North America. Here is how the task is presented to the students in the Social Studies class. The teacher role-plays the executive director of "Go Green."

"As you know, here in Atlanta we are facing growing concern over the expansion of urban areas into rural land that surrounds the city. This urban growth is having a negative effect on farming in our area. Of particular concern is the loss of farmland as developers look for the easiest places to build new subdivisions. We have wanted to alert the people of Atlanta to this issue for some time. However, getting funding for any kind of public awareness campaign has been a real problem. In looking for sources of funds, the directors of this agency have contacted another environmental group in Denver called 'Save The Planet'; its members are concerned about similar land-use conflicts in their city. Our two agencies have agreed to share the cost of developing a Web site that will raise public awareness of urban/rural land-use issues. The theme of the site will be 'The Tale of Two Cities.'"

"The folks in Denver have slightly different concerns than we do here in Atlanta. Their focus is on the impact that urban development is having on wild animal habitat. Because both organizations want their issue addressed on the site, we want you to compare and contrast the issues surrounding urban growth in both of these cities. You will each be working with a biologist from the Denver organization. I will provide each of you with his or her e-mail address and MSN chat line ID. We need you to contact the biologist right away and get working on developing the Web site. We want the site to be completed in three weeks. Since we have never worked with another agency on this kind of joint project before, our directors are concerned about making sure the other agency holds up its end of the deal. Please keep copies of all communication between you and your partner so we can ensure that the work is being shared."

Students in the Science class are given a similar presentation from the perspective of the people working in Denver. The teacher can arrange for students to have partners in different classes at the same school or at different schools.

PROGRESSIVELY WITHDRAWING FROM HELPING STUDENTS

Six Ways to Teach for Independent and Higher Learning

1. We must resist the temptation to "tell."

2. We must stop teaching decontextualized content.

3. We must stop giving students the final product of our thinking.

4. We must make a fundamental shift—problems first, teaching second.

5. **We must progressively withdraw from helping students.**

I think there is a strong parallel between preparing a young person for adult life in public school and teaching a child to walk. Children learning to walk do not have the leg strength, the coordination, or the sense of balance needed to walk on their own, so parents hold on to their hands tightly in order to catch them when they fall. As children progress, parents gradually loosen their grip on the children's hands. Eventually, parents let go altogether as the children begin walking on their own. Similarly, when students begin school in kindergarten, they do not have the skills or life experience necessary for success in the adult world. At this stage teachers "hold on to their hands tightly" by giving students direction in everything they do. But as students get older and progress in their skill development and life experience, teachers must "loosen their grip" so that students can walk on their own out of school and into adult life. Whether it is a parent teaching a child to walk or a teacher preparing a student for life, the goal is independence for the young person.

Unfortunately, much of our current approach to instruction does not foster independence in students. On the contrary, it makes students dependent on teachers to tell them what they need to know, what they need to do, and how they need to do it. The press of an ever-expanding curriculum creates a focus in the classroom on teaching to the test whether it's the next unit test, grade-wide test, or state/province-wide standardized test. Teachers "hold tightly on to the hands" of their students so they can get them to absorb content long enough to recall it for the exam. But like my student Lisa, pupils forget most of the specific details in short order. Richard Saul Wurman refers to this gorging on information for the sole purpose of regurgitating it as "informational bulimia" (Wurman,1989, p. 201). Ian Jukes adds that these bulimic exercises lead to intellectual anorexia. And when the "teach, test, and turf" approach, which is tightly controlled by the teacher, is the primary style of instruction that students receive right up to the end of high school, students are left unprepared to begin their adult life. School skills centered on test taking don't translate into success in the working world.

Holding tightly on to the hands of our students for too long can lead to other negative side effects. Some of these unintended consequences of teaching to the test have long-lasting crippling effects on young people. I believe the worst one is the fear of failure.

The Fear of Failure

I am amazed at the number of students I have encountered who suffer from the fear of failure. It can be absolutely paralyzing. Some try to cover it up with a nonchalant, devil-may-care façade, but underneath, the reason they are unable to apply themselves is because they're afraid of not measuring up. Teachers often overlook this problem, which is a major factor in learning. Fear stifles innovative thought and paralyzes a student's ability to take risks—and risk taking is a key to creativity. Students are often frozen in their tracks because they are afraid someone will laugh at them. And why should we be surprised that they feel this way? Almost everything we do in the school system tells students that failure is bad. Too often in our rush to cover a curriculum, we do not give students a second chance to demonstrate their learning on a particular topic. In so doing, we not only teach them that failure is bad, we crush their self-confidence in the process. What happens if you don't get it right the first time? You're a loser. After all, if the kids who get A's on their report cards can get it right the first time, you must be slow. Is this the way we want to prepare our students for life?

Certainly young people must be increasingly made aware of the harsh realities of the world, but this must be done gradually if we hope to give them the confidence to be the best they can be. When requesting that educators consider the impact of their instructional approach, Ian Jukes asks them to think about teaching children how to walk. Would you give your children just one chance to master this skill? When they fell down after making their first few faltering steps, would you come along and immediately give them a grade—"Susie, all the other kids on the block took five steps before falling, and you barely took two. You are not keeping up. You only get a grade of C– for your walking." Of course you wouldn't treat them in this way! There are two major reasons why you would use a different instructional approach. First, you know it will take time for your child to develop the skill of walking. Giving them one chance to demonstrate mastery would be absurd. Second, in addition to developing the skill of walking, you want your child to develop self-confidence.

Building students' confidence is a critical aspect of instruction that we often overlook in school. In our haste to cover curriculum and test content recall, we frequently don't allow students time to develop confidence in their abilities. I am saddened by how many senior students come into my classes without the confidence to use their skills. Although it is satisfying to be able to coax some of these students into testing their wings, it is also disturbing that the schooling they have received has not developed their self-confidence to a greater extent. One of the greatest sorrows I have as a teacher is knowing that in the press of the daily demands of my job, I may not have recognized a student's need for some encouragement and may have missed the opportunity to build his or her confidence.

To allow my students time to develop skills without the pressure of immediate evaluation, I often give students a practice assignment that will carry little weight when their grade for a course is calculated. Students learn the value of applying themselves in these practice exercises because a similar major task will follow that has a significant impact on their grade. The skills acquired in the practice task empower the students to complete the major task successfully. Knowing that they have determined an effective way to solve a problem on the practice task gives the students more confidence when working on the major assignment that follows. It doesn't matter if they fail on the practice task. In fact, it is probably better for their learning if they do because that gives the teacher a wonderful opportunity to work with students individually on their approach to solving problems. After a student has encountered difficulty accomplishing a task, he or she is often much more open to receiving direction from the teacher on how to go about the task differently. In addition, the teacher can point out that it was the student's initial failure that led the student to the learning necessary to achieve success. We must teach our students the value of failure.

Consider this: Do you learn more from success or failure? Success tells us that nothing needs to be changed, that we are on the right track and that, if we maintain the status quo, we will continue to be successful. Success does not stimulate creative, outside-the-box thinking because success means you already have a winning formula. Bill Gates says in his 1995 book, *The Road Ahead,* that success is a lousy teacher because it seduces people into thinking that they can't lose. Failure, on the other hand, tells us that we are doing something that needs to be changed. Failure presents our minds with a challenge and calls for our problem-solving abilities to spring into action. Failures are like skinned knees—they are painful, but they heal quickly and are learning experiences. An important truth about the nature of learning is that failure is the mother of high-level imaginative thought. Failure stimulates creative, outside-the-box thinking. Failure fosters exactly the kind of thought we aspire to be teaching our students. Failure is a far more powerful teacher than success, and it is critical that educators work hard to remove the negative stigma around failing.

Linked to students' fear of failure is their inability to cope with uncertainty. One cause of this problem is teachers' overemphasis on questions with right/wrong answers in our instruction and on our tests. I am amazed at the number of senior students in my classes who are constantly asking me if they have the "right" answer or if their thinking is following the "right'" track. They seem incapable of working with any uncertainty for fear of being wrong. This fear makes them dependent on their teachers—a serious shortcoming because, in the world outside school, there is no one at your side telling you exactly what to think. In addition, there is often more than one way to do something. And many major decisions are based on incomplete information, in which case sometimes the only way to proceed is by making your best guess.

Consider buying a house. There is no way of accurately predicting which way interest rates will go, and no guarantee you'll get the raise at work you've been hoping for so you can afford a higher mortgage payment. Will a new transit line come through the neighborhood? Will a developer buy the land across the street and build an apartment building? There are more questions than certainties. The only way to proceed is to do the research, then make a decision based on your best assessment of where things are headed. It's the same thing when starting a new business, creating a new product, hiring a new employee, and so on. In so many situations, there are not just right or wrong answers. However, in schools, the right/wrong approach is used almost exclusively. Consequently, students come to believe that the world functions the same way. It is one of the reasons students have such a difficult time adjusting to life after school. The reality they face when entering the world outside the school system is so very different from the school life they have left behind. Unwittingly, with the best of intentions, we are preparing students for a world that does not exist. Worse, overcoming the habit of dependency on teachers that students develop in school can be embarrassing and even debilitating for them when they enter the working world.

So how do we foster independence in our students? As in the case of the parent teaching a child to walk, we need to let go. Just like a parent, it's our job to make ourselves obsolete. Students should no longer need us when they leave the school system. But what exactly does it mean to "let go" of our students? First, we must stop doing things for them. I am a good problem solver, and I love the feeling of satisfaction that comes from helping someone figure out something that had them stumped. Early in my teaching career, I took great pleasure in telling students who were struggling exactly what they needed to do to make something work. I had visions of my students turning to each other and saying, "Who was that masked man?" as I rode off into the sunset. I have now come to realize that I was actually robbing my students of great learning opportunities. Instead of students wrestling with the problem until they came up with a solution on their own, they relied on me to bail them out when they encountered difficulties. I am beginning to learn the value of acting ignorant. Students will always try to get the teacher to give them the answer or solve the problem because it is the path of least resistance. But, if I insist I do not know how to fix their problem, then students are forced to learn how to do it for themselves.

Withdrawal from helping students is most effective when done progressively. It is critical to have a plan for withdrawing from giving students assistance. Teachers can begin by gradually removing learning crutches from their students over the course of a single school year. But there is also a great need for educators to strategize on how this withdrawal can be phased in over a student's entire educational experience from kindergarten to Grade 12. To institute an effective policy of progressive withdrawal, teachers from different grades and even different schools will have to get together and discuss how to increase student independence as pupils move from level to level. Of course, this is much easier said than done. One of the most disturbing observations I have made of the school system is the lack of communication between teachers. Teachers are often unaware of what the teacher down the hall is doing, let alone what teachers are doing in other subjects, grades, or schools. There is a remarkable amount of compartmentalization in schools. Implementing a systemwide instructional scheme will be a challenge.

REEVALUATING EVALUATION

Six Ways to Teach for Independent and Higher Learning

1. We must resist the temptation to "tell."

2. We must stop teaching decontextualized content.

3. We must stop giving students the final product of our thinking.

4. We must make a fundamental shift—problems first, teaching second.

5. We must progressively withdraw from helping students.

6. We must reevaluate evaluation.

Tom Peters captured it best when he said, "What gets measured, gets done" (Peters, 1986). This simple truth applies to all human endeavor, whether it is in business, education, or personal life. People respond when they are held accountable for their actions. All teachers know that students pay greater attention to the quality of their work when they know they will be graded on an assignment. Evaluating student work is clearly a necessity, but the question is, what do we evaluate?

Currently, much of the evaluation in schools is done with written tests that are based on the content laid out in the standards set by a state or province. Ultimately, students take standardized tests created by the state or provincial department of education. These tests ensure that there is uniform instruction on basic course material throughout the school system. Student performance on these tests is published for all to see. The popularity of this kind of evaluation is growing because standardized tests give parents, politicians, businesses, and the general public a sense of increased accountability in the education system. Due to the importance placed on student performance on these tests, teachers modify their teaching practices to ensure they are covering the material that will be tested—which is reassuring for those in charge of the system and for those who have to pay for it.

However, there is concern about what kind of learning these tests really measure and whether or not they provide a complete picture of a student's learning. Many of the questions on standardized tests are multiple-choice questions. Although these evaluative tools measure certain aspects of learning, they generally test lower-level information recall. It is critical that we not place too great an emphasis on how students perform on these tests because they are not a comprehensive measure of student learning. David Thornburg uses the following fictional example to show that students can actually perform well on the tests we give in our classrooms without having learned anything useful at all. Read the following paragraph about turgium and then answer the questions that follow:

Turgium is the essential component of traduchial fillustrators. Raw turgium is extracted from franzinite, which is mined and refined in Cresepia. The Cresepians use a refinement process that extracts pure turgium from franzinite through the murching process first developed by Fresman and Shnartzer. There is little question that turgium will be a principal factor in the economic growth of Cresepia in the 21st century.

Questions:
1. What is an important use for turgium?
2. Where is turgium found?
3. How is it extracted?
4. How important is it to the economic growth of Cresepia? (D. Thornburg, personal communication, October 17, 2002)

You can answer every one of the questions correctly and still have no idea what turgium really is. Students regularly answer correctly on the tests we give them but have no real understanding of the material. Without a context for how information can be used, the learning that takes place is for the sole purpose of answering a test question correctly. Furthermore, once the task of remembering information for the test has been accomplished, the specific information is forgotten. Everyone I talk to can remember an example of this kind of low-level, short-term information recall from their school experience. My best personal example occurred in Geography 12. In this course, we studied the countries of every continent on the planet. Students were responsible for remembering all sorts of facts about each country we examined. What I find remarkable about my experience in that class is that I have forgotten virtually all the specific information I was taught. Memorizing the material for the tests was a hoop I jumped through to get an A in the course. Without a context to add meaning to the information, it was learning without substance and instantly forgotten. Like all students, I learned how to get the right answer without really knowing what I was talking about. This is not a helpful real-world skill; it's one that will be of little use to students when they leave the school system.

Test scores do not give a complete picture of what students are capable of accomplishing in their schooling. Dave Master (1999) uses the following analogy to make this point. His wife, a nurse, has told him that you can get a good idea of someone's health by measuring their height and weight. But, Master then asks, would you go to a doctor who did only those two measurements when assessing your health? Of course not. You would expect a complete picture of your health to involve much more than determining how tall you are and how much you weigh. You would also want your physician to check your heart rate, measure your blood pressure, check your cholesterol, check your white blood cell count, check your eyesight, do a urine analysis, check your body for areas of pain or discomfort, feel for unusual lumps, check your hearing, listen to your breathing, and perform a number of other tests depending on your age and any unusual symptoms present. Only then would you have confidence in what the doctor had to say about the state of your health. Similarly, we must measure student learning in multiple ways if we hope to get a complete picture of student competence. Like making an assessment of a person's health based only on height and weight, it is quite possible for a teacher to misjudge the capabilities of students by assessing them solely on the basis of test scores.

Although written tests have their place in education, they give only part of the picture. Consider the kind of testing that takes place when someone applies for a driver's license. A written test enables the licensing bureau to determine whether applicants have mastered the basic theory of driving a car and the laws of the road. However, a written exam does not provide enough information to enable those in the motor vehicle office to confidently award a driver's license to an applicant. Ability to recall theory does not mean that someone is ready to be turned loose on the road; the applicant also needs to demonstrate the ability to apply the theory learned to actually driving a car. In the same way, our testing of students at school must not end after giving them a written exam. If our goal is for students to have skills that will enable them to succeed in the world outside the classroom, we must also ask them to demonstrate their ability to apply what they have learned to real-world tasks. There are a variety of ways beyond written exams for students to demonstrate their comprehension of a subject. Teachers can evaluate portfolios of student work. Students can demonstrate their ability to perform certain tasks in timed exercises. Students can do real-world work—for example, create a Web site for a company, build a desk, publish a magazine, cater a banquet, write and produce a play, do a small house renovation, and so on. Unfortunately, these kinds of evaluation seem to be diminishing, not increasing, in schools today.

What I find most disturbing about the current focus on standardized testing is that the evaluative "tail" is wagging the instructional "dog" in education. In other words, because performance on written tests based on content standards is the only measurement that is given any real weight when assessing a student's learning, the amount of time spent on instruction in other skill areas is actually dropping. Teachers can't afford to take time away from teaching what is being measured. This is of great concern because performance on standardized tests is a school skill that does not transfer to the real-world environment. I see students leaving high school today who excel in their ability to perform on written tests yet would not be able to hold a job because they couldn't problem-solve if their lives depended on it.

In addition, we need to make sure that we are not giving students a distorted view of reality using evaluation instruments that focus exclusively on right or wrong answers. As previously discussed, written exams that focus on content foster the idea that there is one correct answer to a question. In most areas of their lives, however, students will discover that there are many right answers to the questions they encounter. They may come up with several ways to get a job done; some solutions may be more efficient, whereas others are more economical. Often the solutions that are more efficient are more expensive. The best solution may likely be a compromise.

We simply need to do a better job of evaluating student learning if we expect students to be able to step out of our classrooms and be successful in the world of work. We must resist the pressure to redefine education as simply teaching to standardized tests; although knowledge of content is certainly important, it is by no means a complete education. Standardized tests are certainly not going to go away, but that doesn't mean we have to view students' performance on those tests as the whole story. We must look for ways to evaluate students doing real-world, higher-level thinking. For students to have productive information recall when they enter the working world, we must teach them to understand the meaning of the facts they memorize and help them learn how to apply this knowledge to do useful things. This means our method of evaluation should give us a picture of a student's ability to analyze, synthesize, and evaluate information to determine its validity and significance. Furthermore, our evaluation needs to give us an assessment of a student's ability to solve problems.

CHAPTER THREE

Teaching Students How to Solve Problems

"**I**f you give a man a fish, you feed him for a day. But if you teach a man to fish, you feed him for a lifetime." This old saying illustrates the significant difference between the value of process and content—the skill of fishing (process) remains useful long after a single fish (content) has been eaten. Processes empower people far more than specific content.

We immediately recognize the truth in this saying. As educators, we need to begin applying this truth more often in our classrooms. In the early grades especially, we are familiar with teaching process skills in a number of areas. When we teach students to read, write, and do arithmetic, we are actually equipping students with process skills. We don't just teach students how to read a single word or a story; we teach them the process of reading to empower students to go on and read an infinite variety of material. We don't just teach students how to write a particular story or an essay; instead, we teach them the process of writing so they can go on and write myriad communications ranging from letters to lab reports. Likewise, we don't just teach students how to add up a single column of numbers; we teach them the process of adding so they can go on and do calculations they have never encountered before. The power is in the process. Even if the specifics change, the process remains valid.

We should be careful, however, not to think that the tried-and-true process skills of reading, writing, and arithmetic comprise the complete set of process skills that students require for life today. Teachers must consider adding another equally important process skill if we hope to give our students all that they will need to survive in the world of the 21st century. To equip young people with the thinking skills that will enable them to apply their learning to real-world situations, we must also embrace teaching the process of problem solving. What young people need when they begin solving problems is a general step-by-step process to follow that will empower them to tackle any sort of problem. In the next section, I outline the four essential steps that will enable anyone to successfully arrive at a solution to a problem. Then, I discuss five process skills that the problem-solving approach encompasses: time management, project management, research, project design, and teamwork. Lastly, I discuss new ways of evaluating students and how to make the transition to the problem-solving mode of teaching.

THE 4 Ds OF PROBLEM SOLVING

The idea of using a structured process for solving problems is not new. At the university level, classes in Systems Analysis and Design outline procedures for solving problems in great detail. I call the problem-solving process I have developed for my classes "the 4 Ds." There is nothing radically new about my approach—I have simply distilled the minimum number of steps for solving a problem out of the process that is commonly taught in post-secondary study.

I discuss the 4 Ds in detail in a moment, but first I want to point out that the role-playing approach for presenting tasks to students discussed in the Chapter 2 goes hand in hand with teaching the 4 Ds. Often, when I am playing the role of a business-person, I do not provide all the details necessary for the students to successfully solve a particular problem. They need to ask questions to get more information. Let's take a look at how this works.

Let's say that a teacher must teach her students about the history of the local area at the turn of the 20th century. When students come into class one morning, the teacher gives them the following presentation to set the scene for the students' task for the day.

"You are going to be architects today. In just a moment, you will be meeting with the manager of a local hotel who has asked to see you about a proposal for a new building project," says the teacher. She then walks out of the room, waits for a few seconds, and then walks back into the classroom as the role-play person.

"Good morning, my name is Ms. Walters, and I am the manager of the Chelton Inn. We have recently purchased a large parcel of land adjacent to our existing hotel, and we want to create a tourist attraction to go along with our new renovation. Our idea is to create a full-size replica of our town's main street as it was at the turn of the 20th century. We would like to know the kinds of businesses that existed at that time as well as any residences in the town at that time. We would like to see any photographs of buildings and town maps. We are also interested in the people who lived here and their backgrounds. We would like recommendations for what the street replica should look like. Please submit a printed report to us in two weeks."

After Ms. Walters has finished talking, it is now up to the students to solve the problem. Without guidance, however, most students will flounder as soon as the teacher sits down. To be able to handle tasks that are presented in this manner, students need to be taught a structured process to follow that will enable them to solve these kinds of real-world problems. Before they begin tackling the solution to the problem, however, they need to obtain more specific information. This leads us to the first "D" of problem solving: Define.

Step One: Define

This is without a doubt the most important step when facing a new task. Think of times when someone jumped to conclusions, causing them to do some good work solving the wrong problem. How many people do you know who took their car to a mechanic only to get their car back with something other than the real problem being fixed? How often do students invest considerable energy in completing a project not according to specifications? Jumping to conclusions is one of the most common difficulties people face when beginning to work on a new task. A great deal of time and effort could be saved if people took the time to properly define a problem before they started working on it.

Consider the problem Ms. Walters presented. Does she want the design for the city street to be historically accurate, or can a number of interesting buildings be grouped together? Should students keep in mind cost considerations when designing the city street? Will tourists be limited to walking down the street, or will they be entering the buildings as well? If they will be going into the buildings, do the buildings' interiors need to be historically accurate as well? How much land can be used for the city street? Does Ms. Walters want rough sketches for the street design in two weeks, or does she want blueprints as well? It is important to nail down these details before starting to work on the solution.

One of the beneficial aspects of this kind of "give students a problem to solve" approach is that students are given only a partial picture of something that needs to be done, which is the way most problems are encountered in real life. They don't come in a neat package with everything already thought out and defined. A complete picture of a problem is formed by gleaning information from conversations, meetings, and firsthand experience. Successful problem solvers learn to ask probing questions to get the necessary details. They also learn to deal with incomplete information and to make judgments based on their best guess at solutions. We must resist the temptation to do most, if not all, of the groundwork for students in the projects we assign. In life, tasks come in a more hazy form, and students will be ill-equipped to handle this reality unless we start making them learn how to dig for the information they require.

The goal of the Define step in problem-solving is to create a list of specifications that outlines all the details that someone needs to know to be able to successfully complete a task. These details must include existing conditions as well as specifications for any new work to be done. Often, this task is one of translation. The person with the problem may not have the expertise to solve the problem alone, which is why the assistance of the students is being requested. Thus, the job of defining the problem involves taking the words and ideas from the person who has the problem and translating them into precise technical terms that the person solving the problem will understand. The details must be written clearly enough so that a person who was not present during the original presentation of the problem would be able to understand the problem and be able to design an appropriate solution.

Problem definition is nitpicking work. To do the job correctly, it is necessary to nail down all of the details. Writing out all of the specifics for a problem is not a very exciting enterprise. I have found that students have a strong tendency to zoom through this step because they want to get on with the "real work" of implementing the solution. However, it is critical that students understand the importance of problem definition if they hope to do well in the world outside school. Furthermore, it is not enough for people to understand the nature of a problem in their minds; they must also be able to document the specifications for a job with enough detail and clarity so that people joining the task midstream can be brought up to speed quickly. People might come and go over the course of a project for many reasons. Someone may get sick or hurt or experience personal difficulties. Someone may be fired or leave for a new job. If any one of these departing people has project details only in his or her own mind, then the success of the work could be significantly delayed, diminished, or even prevented by the lack of information available to replacement workers. Although the job of defining a problem can be tedious, it is an essential step that young people must be taught if they are going to be ready for the world outside school.

An important part of defining a problem is confirming that you have understood the scope of the problem. No matter how well you have listened or taken notes, it's virtually impossible to comprehend and remember everything that was said in a single meeting. That is why you must confirm the details of a new task before you continue. I insist that students get my signature (or the signature of the role-play person) on their problem definition before they move on.

The inclusion of a Define step in the problem-solving process has three major benefits:

• The Define step addresses a major aspect of human nature: people love to procrastinate. Any teacher will tell you that this is a huge problem for students. They commonly leave their work to the last minute, often not beginning to work on a big essay or project until the day before it is due. However, when students are required to define a problem before commencing on the main body of work on a task, it forces them to confront their natural tendency to leave things to the last minute. Instead of starting on a project right before it is due, students must begin doing work on the task at the time it is assigned. To ensure that students get into this habit, I tell them that the role-play person will be available only for the first two periods of the project. Any questions they need answered will have to be asked during that time. I stress that after the role-play person is gone, I cannot answer questions for which only the role-play person knows the answers. When the teacher uses this strategy, students learn that they must begin work on a project right away or they will lack the information they need to successfully complete the assignment. I can easily determine which students are procrastinating by noting the date they bring their problem definitions to me for signing.

• The Define step forces students to learn the value of taking into account how they are going to be rewarded for their work. In the business world, no one would start working on a new task without knowing what a project is worth. Yet I have watched students do hours of work on an assignment without knowing how many marks it is worth. I have also watched teachers decide on the grading criteria after students have handed in their work and the teacher is looking at a stack of assignments to evaluate. Consequently, in many cases, students really have no idea how assignments are marked or why they received a particular grade on a project. Students should know up front the weight that will be given to the various parts of an assignment and what percentage the project will be of their final grade. When I do consulting work, I never begin without first determining how much I am going to be paid. Although we don't pay our students in dollars, we do reward them with grades. Marks should not be undervalued because they can be cashed in for scholarships and, ultimately, jobs. Requiring students to bring their problem definitions to me for signing allows me to check to see whether they have asked for and understood the grading criteria for the project before they begin working on it.

• Another real-world aspect of the Define step is that it gives leverage to the person doing the work rather than to the one asking for the work to be done. I ask my students if they think that in my consulting business I would buy an airline ticket for a job, make a hotel reservation, rent a car, and then arrive in another city without having assurance that the client was going to pay me. Without a contract, a businessperson is powerless to seek any remedy if someone fails to live up to his or her part of a bargain—that is, the businessperson has no leverage with the other party. This leads to a discussion of the issue of leverage and accountability.

> "Tell me, who has all the power in my classroom?" After a short pause I say emphatically, "I do! As a teacher, I ask the questions in the classroom, assign the homework, make the tests, give the grades, give the detentions, and send students to the office. I can greatly affect your lives. So," I then ask, "how would you like to have power over me?" They are always eager to hear what I have to say next. "It's simple. All you have to do is completely define the tasks I give you in this class, including how you will be evaluated, and bring that document to me for my signature. If your definition is complete and correct, I'll sign it and we have a deal. Then, when you hand in your work, if the project is done according to the specifications laid out in the definition, you will not only be able to determine what grade you should get, you'll be able to make me give it to you. Because the criteria for evaluation is in the problem definition that I signed, if I don't give you the grade you feel you deserve, just take the project and the definition that bears my signature to the principal and have him tell me to change your grade."

When I use this explanation, students quickly learn the power of completely defining a task and confirming their definition before going any further.

The form I ask students to use for the Define step of problem solving is shown in Figure 3.1. I have found it a valuable tool for helping students see clearly the information that is needed before they begin working on a project.

I'd like to stress two points about the use of this and any other form in this book. First, I do not have students use a form until they have completed at least two or three tasks. The reason is that

Figure 3.1   Sample completed form for the Define step of problem solving

Problem Definition

Name <u>Fred Bloggs</u>

Date <u>Oct 12/05</u>

Project <u>Trans Pacific Trip</u>

Overview

Create a trip itinerary to Kansai region of Japan for 3 people. Also make recommendation for which city for locating branch office. Present findings in computer presentation and in printed form.

Required Specifications

- Trip itinerary for 3 people:
    - 2 days in Kobe, Kyoto, Osaka
    - Flights
    - Local transportation
    - Hotels
    - 2 days of tourist activities (20th century history)
- Presentation to board of directors
    - Outline itinerary and costs
    - Make recommendation for branch office location based
      on port and financial services
- Printed materials
    - Same content as presentation

Optional Specifications

Evaluation Criteria

- Due in two weeks
- Raw research data   - 20 marks
- Trip itinerary   - 20 marks
- Recommendation—branch office   - 20 marks
- Presentation   - 20 marks
- Printed materials   - 20 marks

Signature _____

I want students to recognize they have a need for organizing their information before I suggest the form to assist them. Too often, we don't let students in our classes struggle enough to become aware of their need for some new tool that will make a job go more smoothly. I want students to discover their need for tools. Second, handing out a premade form is giving the students the final product of my thinking. It may be more expedient, but it robs students of a valuable learning experience. So, as much as possible, I ask my students to help design the forms that they will use for the tasks I give them. This not only involves them in thinking about form design, it also gives them an opportunity to develop their technology skills as they produce a professional-quality form.

Step Two: Design

Have you ever noticed that most things you do are done twice? First, you create a mental picture of the completed project. Then, you actually do it. The first step you took was to design the solution for the task in your mind—to put your mind to work constructing a mental picture of the finished work. Envisioning something that does not yet exist begins during the problem definition step. You must then develop a plan for bringing the vision to reality. For example, to solve a water pressure problem, you may envision placing a large water tank on the top of a hill. However, you still have to figure out how to get the tank up the hill and how to configure the piping to make it operational. Determining the steps required to make the new water system work is the plan that makes the idea a reality.

As students design a plan for the solution to a problem, they become aware of skills and knowledge they are lacking. I require students to identify the specific knowledge they will need to implement their plan successfully. As the creator of the problem to be solved, I ensure that the solution requires students to demonstrate they have learned the skills and information that are outlined in the outcomes of my curriculum guide. Thus, I can give students the problem before teaching them anything, with the confidence that they will be led into the material I would previously just tell them. As a result of this new approach, the students discover their need for learning as a natural part of solving the problem. This is a very satisfying aspect of the problem-solving approach to instruction—students end up asking me to teach them the very material I wanted to teach them in the first place!

This reversal of the traditional roles in the classroom, where the students ask the teacher what they need to be taught instead of the teacher telling students ahead of time what they should know, has two huge benefits. First, students begin to take responsibility for identifying and pursuing their own learning. As a teacher, I am simply a resource to be accessed when needed by my students. I tell my classes that my goal is to teach them only what they ask me to teach. I then make sure the problems I have crafted for my students will lead them into the material they need to learn. As the students discover the need for new skills or knowledge, I discuss with them various sources of learning and which one is best, given the constraint of the timeline for completion of their project. Often groups of students or the entire class decides that the most efficient way to learn something is to have me teach them. Thus, many of the lessons that occur in my courses could be classified as traditional instruction—me up at the front of the room lecturing with the aid of a white board or an overhead projector. There is, however, a significant difference in what happens in my classroom now from what used to take place before I adopted the problem-solving approach. When I am finished teaching a specific concept or skill, I ask the students, "Did I answer your question?" If they say yes, I sit down. I get up again to teach only if one or more of them asks me another question. Thus, the students have much more control of the learning that takes place in the classroom. I set the criteria for the problem and the timeline for completion, and they create the plan for accomplishing the task, including determining the learning they require to get the job done.

Second, by having each student identify the learning he or she needs individually, I can provide differentiated instruction in my classroom that fits with Howard Gardner's (1983) work on multiple intelligences. I do not have to use the traditional "one size fits all" approach, where I tell the same thing to all thirty students in the room, even though many of them have already learned this material. Instead, those students who have already learned a particular skill or acquired certain information can move on to other work while I address just those who are in need of this particular instruction. And some students may choose not to have me teach them the material because they have a different learning style, or perhaps they know someone else who can provide them with the information they need.

Have you ever had a great idea that seemed like the perfect solution to a problem, only to discover the idea was severely flawed when it was actually tried? This is a common experience because our brains are great at imaginative thinking but often stumble when required to think through the specifics of a task logically and sequentially. It is therefore important that we get our ideas checked for flaws in our thinking before we invest too much time and effort in trying to make them work. This is the reason that I ask my students to lay out on paper the logical sequence of steps they intend to follow to accomplish the task they have been given. Creating this Design document allows someone else to look over their plan before work begins. I suggest to my students that they take their plans to be checked by anyone who has experience relevant to their project. Sometimes students bring their plans to me. Sometimes they go to other teachers, to fellow students, to parents, to older siblings, or to someone in the community for feedback. Some students may go to online chat rooms to ask for assistance. I am not concerned about who checks their thinking as long as they have their plans confirmed by someone with knowledge in the appropriate area. It is important to get students in the habit of confirming their thinking before they begin doing their work. This step becomes more critical as the problems students solve increase in complexity.

I have already mentioned that students often find it difficult to start work on a project when it is assigned and to work consistently on it over a period of time instead of leaving most of the work to the last few days before the deadline. I believe a major reason for procrastination is that students are overwhelmed by the scope of a task—the size of major projects can be paralyzing. The key to overcoming this inertia is to get students to break large tasks into a logical sequence of smaller subtasks. This strategy makes a major assignment much easier to tackle. Instead of becoming immobilized at the thought of having to complete a huge project, the student can simply begin on the first, much more manageable, subtask. In addition, as students break the project into smaller units, they can more easily determine which resources and learning will be needed to complete each task successfully.

The form I ask students to use for designing the solution to a problem is shown in Figure 3.2. Again, I do not give the form to the students on the first few problems they solve. I wait until they

Figure 3.2   Sample completed form for the Design step of problem solving

Solution Design

Name <u>Fred Bloggs</u>

Date <u>Oct 13/05</u>

Project <u>Trans Pacific Trip</u>

Subtasks
- Call travel agent and search Internet for the following information for Kobe, Kyoto, Osaka:
    - Flights
    - Hotels
    - Local transportation
    - Tourist activities
    - Port and financial services
- Create trip itinerary
- Formulate recommendation for branch office location
- Create computer–based presentation
- Create printed materials

Resources Needed
- Phone
- Computer with Internet access
- Software:
    - Internet browser
    - Word processor
    - Presentation program
    - Page layout program
- Projector for presentation
- Color printer

Learning Needed
- How do you use Google to find local transportation info for Kobe, Kyoto, and Osaka?
- How do you take images from the Internet and place them on slides in a presentation?
- How do you make points in a presentation appear when the mouse is clicked?

have discovered their need for a tool such as this to assist them. Also, I do not give out ready-made forms to the students; instead, we design them together.

Any good design for the solution to a problem includes a plan for the use of time. To be successful when solving complex problems, students need to assess the amount of time that each step will take and set intermediate deadlines for completing each of the subtasks. Setting intermediate deadlines is critical if students are going to effectively use all of the time allocated for the entire task. Setting intermediate deadlines helps procrastinators to be more aware of the passing of time long before the final deadline arrives. In addition, if students pass an intermediate deadline without completing a subtask, they learn not to waste time because they begin to realize missed work must be made up in the time remaining.

My students use the Design timeline form shown in Figure 3.3 for planning and monitoring their use of time. The time allocated for each subtask is shown as a hollow horizontal bar stretching from the beginning date to the ending date. Students fill in these bars as the tasks are completed. Work done before the intermediate deadline is colored in blue or black. Time spent completing the task after the deadline is colored in red. This color-coded information is especially useful when students come to Step 4, the Debrief step of the problem-solving process.

The timeline is a valuable tool when students are working on a task in groups. Team members may start projects with an understanding of what each person will be contributing, but they can soon lose track of everyone else's progress but their own. Having each member of the team fill in a timeline form as subtasks are completed gives the group a picture of current progress on the project.

It is human nature to want to start work on a project without doing the Define and Design steps. At first, they seem like unnecessary additions that simply add extra work to a task. Even though students might often complain about the additional work you are asking them to do, especially when the assignments are small, it is critical that you persevere. As problems increase in complexity, the Define and Design steps become essential. When students grasp the importance of these steps in solving problems, they see that the work done at the beginning of a new project is critical for ensuring the success of the entire enterprise.

Figure 3.3   Sample completed Design timeline

Timeline Sheet

Project ___Trans Pacific Trip___   Team Members _____

Subtask Timeline

Subtask	Month	October												
	Day	13	14	15	16	17	18	19	20	21	22	23	24	25
• Call travel agent and search Internet for:														
– Flight info			▓	▓	▓	▓								
– Hotel info			▓	▓	▓	▓								
– Local transportation			▓	▓	▓	▓								
– Tourist info			▓	▓	▓	▓								
– Port and financial services info			▓	▓	▓	▓								
• Create itinerary							▓	▓						
• Formulate recommendation														
• Create presentation										▓				
• Create printed materials											▓			

Step Three: Do

After students define the problem and create a design to solve it, it's time for them to put their plan into action. The key is to follow the design, using it as a blueprint for doing the work. Students often remark that doing the actual work on a project is anticlimactic. In many ways, this is how it should be, because the critical thinking ought to be done in the Define and Design steps of the problem-solving process. When implementing their ideas, some adjustments may be needed, but if the definition is accurate and the design is sound, actually doing the task should be straightforward. I tell students that the work of putting a project together in the Do step should be a confirmation of their thinking. However, if they encounter difficulties at this stage, I stress that this does not mean their work up to this point has been a waste of time. Quite the contrary—learning from our mistakes is an important step on the road to success.

The Do step may seem anticlimactic, but that doesn't mean the teacher can sit back and relax. In fact, you may need to do a lot of hard work during this step. I have observed that many teachers are not as actively involved in this stage of a project as they are at the beginning and at the end; teachers often just let students work. This is a mistake. Students often have difficulty working on a task consistently through to completion. For students to learn the skill of time management, they must be monitored throughout the duration of a project. I ask students to refer to their timeline sheet and continually update their project timeline. I do spot checks to monitor whether students are on target as outlined on their timeline sheet. For group projects, I ask groups to meet with me on a weekly basis to discuss their progress. The timeline sheet is a focal point for group discussions. The group may need to adjust its intermediate deadlines and reallocate group members to those tasks that are proving to be more time consuming than originally expected. They can also reallocate work from group members who are absent. The timeline sheet is an excellent tool for both the teacher and the student when it comes to monitoring individual and group progress on a task.

The product that students produce in the Do step can take many forms. Students could be working on the most common assignments in school, such as writing a report, writing an essay, or doing a lab write-up. They could be doing any number of other things as well—performing in a play, creating a sculpture, making a Web site, building a desk, filming a movie, preparing a meal, doing a multimedia presentation, participating in a debate, and so on and so on. Whatever it is that they do, students should see the final product as an expression of their thought process. In the classroom, we must not focus solely on the end product; rather, we must help students to view the Doing as the culmination of the process of Defining and Designing.

Step Four: Debrief

Debriefing is simply assessing how well a student did on a project. However, debriefing is more than the traditional assessment done solely by the teacher after a project has been completed. Debriefing is an assessment done jointly by the teacher and the student. Such assessment is a valuable part of learning. The purpose of the debriefing step is to recognize which parts of the assignment the student did well and to offer constructive criticism on what could have been done better. The goal is improved performance the next time the student does a similar task.

Debriefing a person's work is a very important part of business strategy because it helps workers progress in their ability to do various tasks. As employee skill increases, so does company productivity. Debriefing is not meant to be a punitive experience. If something went wrong, then it is important to find out why so it won't happen again. If a job was well done, the workers responsible are congratulated by their boss and/or fellow team members. This kind of assessment of employee performance is an integral part of a company's development in the business world.

Yet, debriefing is missing from much of the evaluation that we do in education. We give students a grade for their work, but we have a tendency to move on to new work without much discussion of how well the previous report, essay, or project was done or how it could be improved. In our haste to get through a subject, we often miss valuable learning opportunities with our students. We give students the idea that you have only one opportunity to do something in life, and then you move on without assessing how things went. An unfortunate consequence of the "get a grade and move on" approach to evaluation is that students wash their hands of responsibility for their work after they hand it in to the teacher.

I have had many students plunk down a completed assignment on my desk and declare with great satisfaction, "I'm done!" They are shocked if I ask them to take it back to complete missing parts of the assignment or if I challenge them about the quality of their work. I even had one student tell me that it wasn't his job to evaluate his work, it was mine! In discussions with my colleagues, I have found that this attitude is not uncommon. Over the years, I have come to see that the reason students do not take ownership for the quality of their work is due largely to the fact that teachers do not take the time to debrief students' work with them.

It took me quite a while to catch on. I had been teaching for many years before I realized that my approach toward evaluation was a major reason that students took so little responsibility for their work. Students in my classes had learned that working on school-related tasks I gave them was a linear process. Their responsibility for a project began when I assigned it and ended when they handed it in to me. Then, I took their assignments home with me and, completely out of sight of the students, I came up with a grade for their work. And because of the pressure to completely cover my curriculum, I rarely revisited assignments— I just moved on, and students had to live with whatever grade was given them. No wonder the students in my classes didn't take much ownership for the quality of their work; I never made them examine their work critically or had them justify why they thought they deserved a certain grade. I did all the assessment out of sight and rarely gave them any feedback beyond the mark I put on their work.

I realized I needed to change the way evaluation took place in my classroom. It dawned on me that the specifications of the problem that the students had detailed in the Define step could be used as a tool to assess the quality of the completed project. I began telling my students to return to their Define document before handing in their completed projects to evaluate whether their finished work met all of the criteria outlined there. I also asked students to give their work a grade based on how well they thought they had done.

Requiring my students to critically analyze how well a project has met the criteria determined in the Define step has resulted in three significant benefits. First, my students have become much more aware of the quality of their work because I do not allow them to hand in a project without them first making an assessment of what they think their work is worth. Most students have responded by producing better work. Students have also responded with quite realistic assessments of what mark they should receive for a project. I have found, with only a few exceptions, that when given the chance, students are not only very honest in assessing their work, they are also very accurate. If anything, most students are much harder on themselves than I am.

Second, by having them return to the criteria set out in the first step of the process, students see problem solving as a cyclical process instead of a linear one. This circularity mirrors the reality in the world outside school, where work can be revisited several times to produce the highest quality product. When students are required to return to the original specifications for a task, they become aware of the shortcomings in their final product. Students often come to me after debriefing their work to ask for more time to "re-Do" a part of a project because they have realized they have not met all of the criteria set out in the Define document. This, in turn, leads them to revisit the Design work they have done on the project. This cycling again through the 4 Ds is exactly what students need to embrace as the normal way of solving problems.

Third, student participation makes evaluation a much more transparent process. Students can now see how a grade is determined, partly because they do the first assessment themselves and partly because my confirmation of their self-evaluation is not final. If I do not agree with some aspect of their evaluation, it becomes a source of dialogue. In this dialogue, I encourage students to argue for what they think their grade should be and to back that up by showing me how they have met the criteria for the project. This kind of discussion with a teacher can be intimidating for many students. I tell them that the ability to overcome their insecurities and to use logic to argue for what they believe is right is an important life skill that they must develop. In our dialogue, students learn why I think their work does not measure up to the specifications for a task, which can help them do better on subsequent projects. However, if a student can convince me that my assessment of his or her work is not correct, I am happy to change the grade. The student is pleased with the higher mark, but I am more pleased because I have encouraged the student to approach me with concerns and to cogently lay out an argument. This dialogue over evaluation has been a very positive addition to my classroom.

TEACHER EVALUATION OF PROCESS SKILLS

Getting students to take responsibility for doing the initial evaluation of their work was a huge step forward in fostering independence in my students. However, some major frustrations in my teaching remained. I found that students were repeating the same mistakes over and over on subsequent assignments. This tendency became more pronounced as the tasks became more complex. The longer I looked at the difficulties students were encountering, the more I realized it was the process of doing their work that was causing them trouble. I, like many teachers, however, was focused on evaluating the end product of their work. I needed to shift my focus from exclusively looking at what they did to include looking at how they did it. This realization took me into uncharted waters because process evaluation had never been modeled for me in my own schooling experience. Evaluating the process students use when completing a project has been the biggest challenge for me in teaching students how to debrief their work. To gain understanding, I have had to look beyond educational resources, consulting with people in business and reading business books, because the business world is where I found a concern for the process of how things get done.

I discovered what any savvy businessperson today will tell you—to improve a product, you must first improve the process of producing it. This was the thinking behind the reorganization at Genie Industries, discussed in Chapter 1. My problem was that my focus for evaluation was so narrow, I was missing the process of learning altogether. Talking to other teachers, I have found that this is a common problem. We often fall short in teaching our students because we believe that someone else is teaching them the learning processes required for success. We assume our students know how to do the research, manage their time, and work consistently throughout the duration of a project. However, in my experience, these are faulty assumptions. Students need help developing process skills if they are going to be successful in our classrooms and in the world outside school.

I have determined several key process skills that students must master if they are going to be successful in solving the tasks I give them. Not only will these process skills help them with their schoolwork, but they are also critical skills for success in the world outside school. I ask students to comment on each of the following five areas when debriefing their work: time management, project management, research, project design, and teamwork.

Time Management

Students today are busier than ever before. Many have part-time jobs, and many are responsible for caring for their younger siblings. In addition, many are involved in sports, dancing, youth groups, and a variety of clubs. Many students have difficulty budgeting their time effectively so that they live up to their various responsibilities as well as allow time for recreation. To help with scheduling, I ask students to use a time planner to document their use of time. Some students use the planner that is provided by our school, whereas others design their own using various computer programs. Others use business time planners that are available in stores. I tell students that they can fudge the data in their planner if they want to and I may never know. However, they will miss valuable learning opportunities if they do. Most students complete their planner sheets accurately when they see that I use the information as a positive learning tool, not as a way to make them feel bad about their performance. Having students comment on their use of time has led to some productive discussions about setting priorities. A common problem students have is overcommitment. Some students are simply trying to do too much, and they suffer for it. I tell them they are experiencing the effect of Gerald Weinberg's Law of Raspberry Jam (Weinberg, 1985, p. 11) in their use of time—the more you spread it, the thinner it gets. This causes them to think about setting priorities in the use of their time and to consider how they can reduce the number of activities on their plate.

Time-management difficulties, like difficulties with most process skills, are often invisible unless the teacher digs deeper than just looking at a student's completed project. It is important to note that even students who receive high grades on an assignment might still have time-management problems. The traditional approach of focusing exclusively on evaluating the end product for an assignment will miss this difficulty the student is having. If left undiagnosed, the time-management problem can result in incomplete work on subsequent projects when the workload increases or the timeline is shortened.

Project Management

Many students have difficulty working consistently throughout the entire duration of the time allotted for a project. Some students get off to a good start on long-term projects but let the work slide as time passes. As the deadline approaches, they work feverishly to try and make up for work that should have been done earlier. Some students do not finish the work on time. Others complete the task, but the product they hand in is substandard because they have had to rush their work to finish on time.

The timeline sheet created in the Design step and filled in during the Do step becomes a valuable tool for assessing students' project management. The key is to convince students of the value of filling in the form truthfully. Again, I tell students that they can fudge the data on these sheets to make themselves look good on paper, but if they do, we will not be able to effectively evaluate their project management skills. The timeline sheet not only lays out when various tasks were planned to be done, it also indicates when work on the various subtasks was actually started and how long it took. From this information, it is easy to see some of the common problems students have with the use of their time while doing a project. For example, if a student has put off doing work until the last minute, then the red bars showing when students began the various subtasks for the project will be skewed to the right side of the timeline, close to the deadline. I have found that asking students to analyze when the work on the various subtasks was actually done has been useful in helping them develop better project management skills.

Research

Research skills include the ability to find relevant information for a specific task, the ability to analyze that information to discover its true meaning, and the ability to apply this newfound knowledge to solve the given problem. Another critical research skill that is often overlooked is the ability to first determine what knowledge and skills are needed to complete a project and to take the steps necessary to acquire the required learning. For example, to build a stereo cabinet, students would need knowledge of various woods and wood glues. Students would also need to know how to operate a table saw and an electric drill.

Although research skills should form a foundation for all the work that students do in school, students often arrive in my senior classes without them. Many teachers think that research skills, like other process skills, are taught by someone else. They give assignments and assume that students know how to attack them. I am astonished by how many of my students' difficulties with project completion stem from their lack of effective research skills. Having students comment on their ability to do research leads to discussions about where information is located and how it can be accessed. Further, I often discuss with students strategies for analyzing information to determine its meaning. These are important skills that help students in all their courses. Although many students possess research skills that enable them to gather information, they frequently stumble when it comes to taking responsibility for acquiring the learning needed to do a task. This difficulty is apparent at the beginning of a project, especially when I begin withdrawing from providing all of the instruction needed to accomplish a task. Some students take an inordinate amount of time getting started on a project because they do not know how to determine what they need to learn or where to get that instruction. When I give students assistance in getting started, I ask them to comment on their difficulties in their debrief of the project. When I talk with students after the project has been completed, we discuss how skills can be learned and the best way to learn them given the time available.

Project Design

As mentioned earlier, students are in the habit of having teachers do most of the design work for projects. Consequently, students often struggle when asked to design a plan that will lead to the successful completion of a task. Several common weaknesses are revealed when students debrief the design aspect of their work. Some students neglect to use all the information that was specified in the Define step when developing their design plan because they forget to continually refer back to the Define document during the Design step. Their final product, therefore, is doomed to be less than satisfactory even before actual work has begun because one or more of the specifications in the problem definition are not addressed in the design of the solution. I stress the importance of referring to the Define document throughout the Design step to ensure that the end product is successful in every way.

In addition, many students have trouble setting realistic goals for themselves when planning a project. Every teacher recognizes the underachievers and overachievers in their classes. The overachievers set their sights too high and try to do everything. The underachievers set their sights too low and do as little as possible. Although teachers can detect some of these problems when a student's problem definition is checked, many of these difficulties do not surface until a project is well underway. When students are honest in their debriefings, these areas of difficulty are highlighted and lead to productive discussions about goal setting.

Another area that students struggle with in project design is the development of a logical sequence of subtasks. This difficulty is often one reason that students have trouble getting started on a project. Discussions with students regarding their inability to determine the order of subtasks for a project often reveal students' fear of failure or fear of looking stupid. Rather than risk failure or ridicule, many students simply avoid working on a task. Although I am sure I don't catch all of the students in my classes who suffer from these anxieties, debriefing with my students has led me to discover quite a number who do. Armed with this understanding, I can then work with students individually, often outside class time so that other students cannot see a particular student's struggles.

It is important to stress to students who are encountering difficulties that project design is not easy to master, and the first step to conquering project design is to be able to say, "I don't know how to do that." This is a challenge for students who are products of a system that rewards you for "knowing." However, the ability to acknowledge the limits of their skills and understanding becomes increasingly important as students progress through school.

I stress to students that admitting that you don't know something is the first step in learning. I also point out that it is critical that students quickly recognize the limits of their understanding when they are given projects in other classes. We discuss the fact that many of their teachers assume that students can do the tasks that are assigned. The biggest breakthrough occurs when students can see for themselves that saying, "I don't know how to do that" is a perfectly intelligent thing to say. We talk about the fact that significant discoveries in human history have been made because intelligent people, realizing they didn't know something, had the courage to set out to learn what they didn't know. The key to success is acting on your awareness of "not knowing" by going out and acquiring the skills or the understanding that you lack. Some of the most satisfying teaching I have done has been to help students overcome their fears and to begin to be more confident in tackling assignments that involve overcoming a learning deficiency.

Teamwork

The ability to work well in a group is an important life skill. However, it does not come naturally to many students. Students find the delegation of tasks to group members a challenge because not all subtasks are equal in duration or difficulty. The various personalities of group members and their level of commitment to their studies can create dysfunctional group dynamics. Most teachers who have had their students do group work will recognize these problems. Often, an overachiever takes control of a group and does most of the work, which causes one or more problems. The person doing the lion's share of the work may burn out under the weight of the burden he or she has taken on. This can result in an incomplete or substandard project. Further, even though the overachiever was the one who engineered the delegation of subtasks, he or she can become resentful of other group members who are doing less work. I have also seen a group produce an outstanding product that was primarily the work of a single individual; in this case, other group members who were shut out of the entire process could be upset at their exclusion. Then there are the groups who have difficulties with an underachiever who does not complete the tasks that he or she was assigned.

Regardless of the nature of the dysfunction, the major difficulty that some groups have is that they avoid dealing with the relational problems they are experiencing. Most of the time, these difficulties are addressed in the weekly meetings. However, for some groups, things appear just fine in the meetings while in reality, they are having challenges working as a group. When these group-dynamics problems come to the surface in the debriefs that students submit, I stress the importance of members of a team being honest with one another and dealing with these difficulties when they first arise. Students begin to see that avoidance is not an effective strategy when dealing with team relationships because, invariably, avoidance yields only temporary respite. It allows a problem to grow, making resolution more difficult in the end.

STUDENT EVALUATION OF PROCESS SKILLS

Having students comment on process skills in addition to assessing the quality of the product they have produced provides a much fuller picture of the learning that has occurred on a project. This feedback is valuable to the teacher, but it is even more valuable to the student. Because our goal is independence for our students, it is crucial that students take increasing responsibility for the evaluation of their work. To help students become more accountable for the quality of the work they produce, I ask them to give me an invoice for their grades (see Figure 3.4). In business, no one pays for completed work until they have received a bill. Likewise, I tell students that if they want a grade, they have to give me an invoice for the work they have done. Instead of dollars, students list the marks they think they deserve on each item in the evaluation criteria. (Depending on whether the project is completed early or late in the school year, this evaluation can range from simply assessing how well the items in the Define document were met to also including evaluation of the process skills involved. See the next section for more information.) I tell them to be prepared to justify why they think their work is worth the grade they have given themselves.

Figure 3.4   Sample completed student invoice

Fred Bloggs Consulting Ltd.

21844 - 124th Avenue
Maple Ridge, CA
91324

Invoice

Customer TRANS PACIFIC SHIPPING

Date	Invoice Number	Terms
OCT 25/05		DUE ON RECEIPT

Qty	Item	Maximum	Mark
1	Raw research data	20	18
1	Trip itinerary	20	17
1	Recommendation for branch office	20	14
1	Computer presentation	20	20
1	Printed report	20	18
	Total	100	87

Credit marks to Fred Bloggs

One of the biggest changes in the way that evaluation takes place in my classroom has been the incorporation of a dialogue with students over their grades. Students are encouraged to discuss their concerns over how a grade was determined. This naturally leads to feedback from me regarding the strengths and weaknesses of their work. I believe this dialogue is important in helping students get used to receiving constructive criticism. Often, students are uncomfortable taking criticism and become overly defensive. As is the case with any skill, it takes practice to improve, and the dialogue that arises from debriefing work gives students practice receiving critical comments about what they have done.

PUTTING IT ALL TOGETHER

Like teaching any new skill, employing a problem-solving method of instruction is best done progressively. I start small with modest tasks to allow students to master the basics and build toward larger projects so that, by the end of the school year, students must employ all of the steps of the 4 D process. On the first few assignments, I concentrate on getting the students to master the detective work of defining a task from a role play. On subsequent assignments, I introduce more of the problem-solving process. Because debriefing their work is completely new for most students, I start with very minimal requirements for their first debriefs. To begin with, I ask them to focus on assessing how closely their work comes to meeting the criteria set out in the Define document. I then progress to having students include an assessment of one or two process skills, like time management and project design. After students become comfortable with the 4 D method of doing tasks, I begin requiring more of them while helping them less. Remember, our goal is not just to teach students how to solve problems—we want them to solve problems independently. We cannot simply teach students about the four-step method that can be used to complete a task; we must help them internalize the process so that they learn to apply it without being told. As the year progresses, I begin to hold students accountable for things I do not directly assign. If I have presented them with a new problem to solve, have given them a deadline for getting it done, and have told them how they are going to be rewarded, then I expect that they will apply their knowledge of the 4 D problem-solving process to get the job done. Toward the end of the year, after doing a role-play presentation of a new problem to my students, I expect them to have the Define step completed by the beginning of the next class without me telling them to do so. Furthermore, I do not expect students to stop working on the assignment just because they have finished their Define work. They know the next step is to design a solution, so I expect them to begin working on their design without being told that as well. I follow through by checking on their progress the next time I see them.

A NEW ROLE FOR TEACHERS

Implementing the new problem-solving approach to instruction requires a shift in what teachers do in the classroom. Let's summarize the new roles for teachers. First, teachers must become crafters of problems. I believe this is the most important shift teachers can make in the classroom. It not only involves presenting tasks as real-world problems to be solved, but it means moving away from "telling" as the only way for students to encounter course content. Teachers must have a thorough knowledge of the course curriculum to shape problems that will lead students to learn the required material. In addition, teachers must utilize their imaginations to the fullest to make the learning that takes place in the classroom an engaging experience for students.

Teachers must also make the shift to being process instructors in addition to being content instructors. Processes empower our students to rise to greater heights after they leave us because, although specific content may become obsolete, processes remain valid for a lifetime. For example, equipping our students with the 4 D problem-solving process gives them a life skill with great power because, although the specific problems students face may change over the course of their life after school, the process of solving them will remain the same.

There will always be times when teachers should be at front and center in the classroom, but teachers also need to explore other formats if they hope to engender in students the independence they will need for success. Teachers must embrace the role of guide and begin to see themselves as an instructional resource for students to use as they go about the task of solving problems.

This means that teachers must yield more control of learning to the students and let them take more responsibility for pursuing what they need. There is an element of planned obsolescence in the teacher's new role; the goal is to guide students through the process of solving problems until they can do it on their own without help from the teacher.

Finally, teachers must make the shift in evaluation from being a judge to being a confirmer and challenger. In their new role, teachers confirm and sometimes challenge the assessments students make of their own work. Again, this role involves yielding some of the control in the classroom to the students. This shift should occur progressively as the students become more capable in self-assessment. This change is extremely beneficial because this type of cooperative evaluation motivates students to improve the quality of their work.

A NEW WAY TO EVALUATE

Students can develop problem-solving skills at the same time that they are learning the content laid out in course standards set by the state or province. The key to successfully integrating this new instructional method into the classroom is posing problems that lead students into the required course content. The advantages of this approach are that students develop problem-solving skills that will empower them for lifelong success and that the problem provides a context that helps students later remember the specific content they encountered while solving it.

Evaluating the Process

When we embrace the problem-solving process in our instruction, we must change the way we evaluate students' work. We must evaluate the process as well as the end product. It can be a challenge getting students to focus on anything but the end product of an assignment. There are two major reasons for this. First, the students focus solely on the end product because most of the time, that is all that is marked. Students know that grades are what count in school, and that is where they concentrate their efforts. Second, the teaching and evaluating of process learning is foreign to most people when they become teachers because it has not often been modeled for them in the school system. Therefore, teachers naturally continue to focus on the end product of student learning rather than on the process of learning. However, if we want students to embrace the problem-solving process, we must give marks for more than just the completed report, essay, drawing, sculpture, or other final product. We must also identify key processes in the 4 D procedure for which student abilities can be evaluated.

What I look for when I evaluate students' projects is evidence that they have followed the 4 D process to produce the requested product. Students must create a Define document that is specific and complete. It must include all the evaluation criteria needed for doing their debrief of the finished project. I expect students to develop their own form for defining a task. This document must be signed by me to indicate that they have confirmed their understanding of a task before continuing. For the Design step, students must also develop a form for the following information—the sequence of subtasks, the resources that will be needed to accomplish the task, and identification of any learning that will be required before the project can be completed. In addition, they must create a timeline for the project, including setting intermediate deadlines for completing each of the subtasks. To make sure students know that I am serious about having them do this preparatory work, I give marks for both the Define and Design steps before they begin the Do step.

The primary evidence of the Do step is the product the student produces for the project, but it is important to check that students have followed the plan outlined in the Design step. This connection—between design and final product—will be critical to enable students to successfully complete larger tasks when they leave school. If the product students produce is considerably different from the one planned in their design, this usually indicates that they are leaving most of the thinking until the product is actually being created. Some adjustments to the original design are to be expected, of course, but radical shifts usually indicate a lack of forethought.

A debrief must include an evaluation of the quality of the product that was created. What I look for is an honest and realistic assessment of how well the student has met the criteria for the project set out in the Define document. I require students to rate their performance out of 10 on each of the specifications outlined in the Define step. These marks are itemized on a separate line of the invoice they submit to me. As I have already indicated, when the students become comfortable with the debriefing process, I require that they include an assessment of the process skills they used to produce the project—time management, project management, research, project design, and group work. I usually ask students to rate these areas out of 100 because I have found they are much better at assessing their work in percentage terms. I then take their assessments into account when I determine the grade that is appropriate for the specific project.

Note that when you evaluate a student's process skills, you can award high marks even if the product itself was not outstanding, because the emphasis is on the learning that has taken place. As we have already discussed, significant learning can take place even when a student fails at doing something. In fact, I believe that when I give a student high marks on a project, I am often affirming not the learning the student did on *this* assignment but the learning that took place on a *previous* one. The high grade for the current project simply confirms that the student has been able to successfully apply what he or she learned on previous assignments. Therefore, it is important to reward students when they follow the 4 D process and can identify what went wrong in their debrief of the project. I expect students to outline what they have learned from their failures as well as successes.

However, I will give credit for learning a lesson only once. For example, if a student has indicated he or she has learned not to wait until the end of the time allotted to start working on a project, I expect progress in that area on the next assignment. If the student identifies the same problem in his or her debrief on the next project, I do not give the student credit for learning anything new. Thus, it is important to keep copies of student debriefs for future reference when marking subsequent assignments.

Evaluating Personal Attributes

I have outlined a basic framework for evaluating the 4 D problem-solving process. However, in addition to going beyond content evaluation, I believe that assessment should even surpass process evaluation if we truly want to get students ready for the world outside school. Teachers must also give tangible credit for the personal attributes that are valued in life outside school if we want students to see them as important. What kinds of attributes am I talking about? Think of the attributes you would like to see developed in your own children. Certainly you want them to progress academically, but you also want your children to progress in being reliable, taking initiative, working independently, being polite, having a positive attitude, being honest, and so on. These characteristics are also what employers are looking for when they hire new workers. In fact, these nonacademic qualities are often far more significant in determining a person's advancement in the working world than the grades on a school transcript.

If the development of these qualities is so desirable, why don't we measure them in school? Most teachers encourage students to display qualities such as initiative, self-discipline, respect, and positive attitude in their classrooms. Yet, no matter how much teachers talk about the need for such attributes, they only give marks for assignments and tests. Work habits may be listed on report cards, but students know that grades are what really count. I can think of a number of times I have just been getting into a productive discussion about the merits of developing exemplary personal attributes when the discussion has been brought to an abrupt halt by a student asking, "Is this going to be on the test?" To be able to assure students in my classes that such discussions are truly valuable, I require students to give themselves a grade for their progress in developing two important personal qualities: a positive attitude and independence.

A positive attitude tops my list of valuable personal traits because it has such an enormous impact on those around us. In fact, a person's attitude is perhaps the most powerful force in his or her life. It can ruin relationships or build careers. It can make life difficult for others or make working with someone a real joy. A person's attitude can significantly influence everyone that person meets. I believe the following quote from Chuck Swindoll captures the incredible power of attitude:

> The longer I live, the more I realize the impact of attitude on life. Attitude, to me, is more important than facts. It is more important than the past, than education, than money, than

circumstances, than failures, than successes, than what other people think or say or do. It is more important than appearance, giftedness or skill. It will make or break a company, a home. The remarkable thing is we have a choice every day regarding the attitude we will embrace for that day. We cannot change our past, we cannot change the fact that people will act in a certain way, we cannot change the inevitable. The only thing we can do is play on the one string we have, and that is our attitude. I am convinced that life is 10% what happens to me and 90% how I react to it. (Swindoll, 1982, p. 207)

I want students to assess their positive attitude while working on projects because, as Swindoll points out, people get to choose what their attitude will be. How they react to difficulties and setbacks is one of the few things in life that is in their complete control. Thus, positive attitude rated out of 100 is a separate line on the invoice a student submits to me for a project.

The second personal quality I ask students to assess is independence. I want students to assess their independence because the ability to work on their own will be so important when students leave school. If students have been relying on others to help them get through their schoolwork, they will have developed a very bad habit that can be crippling when they leave the school environment. I encounter far too many students each year who have developed this kind of unhealthy reliance on others. These students are not cheaters; they do the work that is required, but they wait for someone else to go first to show them the way. It's safer to do it this way, of course, and it takes less time and effort than trying to figure something out on your own, but someone else took all the risks and really did all the difficult thinking. The dependent student then came along and followed in that person's wake. Although this strategy makes it easier to complete work done in school, it sets students up for an unpleasant surprise when they meet the expectation of independence in the world of work.

Students often ask me why I evaluate their personal attributes as well as their academic performance, especially because none of their other teachers give grades for developing these characteristics. My response is simple—"You are who you practice to be." I explain to them that it is folly to think they will immediately develop these attributes upon leaving school and entering the work force. So, how do you get better at playing the piano, playing basketball, or developing a positive attitude? Practice. To ensure you are job-ready with the kinds of personal characteristics that employers desire, you must practice them while you are in school.

MAKING THE TRANSITION
TO A NEW TEACHING APPROACH

Let me be up front about the challenge of implementing this problem-solving approach in your classroom. It requires time and energy. It will likely feel uncomfortable because it is not like anything you have seen before in school, university, or teacher training. You may even encounter some resistance from administrators or parents who are focused exclusively on school skills. So why bother? Simply put, it is a professional imperative that we prepare our students for life after school. Eventually, they will have to leave the school system and enter the larger working world, and we must make sure they are ready. That means teaching them problem-solving skills and fostering independence along with teaching them all of the elements of a traditional education.

A challenging aspect of implementing this approach is that the teacher must become a learner. However, this learning can be a positive element in the classroom. As educators, we often talk with our students about the importance of being lifelong learners, and we should model this for them. There is always something new to learn about how to teach effectively, how to create that illusive optimal learning environment for your students. Being a teacher means being a work in progress, and that means that the current reality of your teaching falls short of the ultimate goal. I would love to say that I follow all of the steps outlined in this book on every assignment I give to my students, but it just isn't so. The realities of everyday teaching make it impossible to live up to everything I have laid out here. However, I am striving to implement this approach in more and more classes and on more and more assignments. That is my goal. I may not reach it, but I do my best given the constraints of time and energy. As I say to my students, "the reality of life is often a compromise." But that doesn't mean I can't aim for the moon. Ian Jukes says the trouble in education is not that we aim too high and miss the mark but that we aim too low and hit the target every time. I don't want to become so comfortable with routine that my students lose out because I put my desires ahead of their needs. But working this out each day is not an easy task. I believe that given the press of curriculum and all of the other daily tasks of teaching, continually improving our instructional effectiveness is one of the greatest challenges we face as teachers. I encourage you to keep setting your goals high and doing your best to reach them.

To make the transition to this problem-solving method of instruction easier as well as to increase the chance of its success, I recommend that teachers start making the transition slowly. Be realistic about how much you can implement at one time. Try presenting an assignment in problem form to your students on just one assignment in a term. You may also decide to implement only parts of this approach. For example, on smaller assignments, I often present the task to students as a problem and skip doing a role play. Or I may present the problem in a role-play presentation and have students define the task, but due to the small scope of the assignment, I skip having students create a formal design. After you have gained some comfort with the approach, try implementing the entire 4 D process on a larger task. Then you might try presenting a series of lessons and assignments as problems. The key is to begin moving in a new direction away from the traditional "let me tell you about . . ." approach so your students can develop the problem-solving skills they need. Imagine if every teacher across the curriculum used this problem-solving approach for just one or two assignments per year, how much better prepared our students would be to face the world.

I cannot overstate the importance of simply getting moving toward the goal of teaching students effective real-world problem-solving skills. It doesn't matter if the first steps are small. It doesn't even matter if you find yourself heading off in the wrong direction. The critical thing is to start moving. You will learn soon enough from any missteps and make the necessary adjustments to get back on track. Remember that you cannot steer a parked car! I have not arrived as a teacher. In fact, the longer I work in education, the more I realize there is so much I don't know about this job. The key for me is to keep moving, to continually try new things— learning what works, what doesn't, and then trying again.

PREPARING FOR SUCCESS IN THE 21ST CENTURY: PROBLEM SOLVING, ROLE PLAYING, AND REALITY SIMULATION

With all of the high-tech gadgetry cascading into our lives, you might have thought this book would be about teaching students how to use technology. In my view, the use of technology in the classroom is not the critical issue facing us in education in the 21st century. The issue of foremost importance is to develop thinking skills in our students so that they will be able to utilize the power of technological tools to solve problems and to do useful work. People who possess technology skills but lack independent problem-solving skills are useless until someone tells them what to do. The use of technology needs to be taught along with the higher-level thinking skills required to solve problems. People with these independent problem-solving skills plus technology proficiency will have great power and will be effective, productive participants in families, communities, and businesses.

In many schools, technology is not available in every classroom. Some teachers cite this as the reason they cannot change the way they teach. They believe that technology is the key to preparing students for the new world and that substantive changes cannot be made without it. I do not agree. Modifying instruction in the ways I have outlined in this book can be done in any classroom. You don't need technology to foster higher-level thinking skills. Of course, it is best if students have access to technological tools, but computers and other electronic tools can be accessed outside the classroom if necessary. Even in the increasingly high-tech world of the 21st century, what students need first and foremost are effective thinking skills.

As I have mentioned many times, my goal in using a problem-solving strategy when teaching my students is to get them ready for the real world. The best endorsement of this method of instruction came from one of my students a few years ago. After teaching one of my senior classes using the 4 D problem-solving approach with reality simulation role plays, I felt they were ready to tackle a task in the world outside the classroom. I arranged for the class to travel to Genie Industries in Redmond, Washington, to meet with the human resources manager. He was in need of a fairly complex Web site to disseminate a wide range of information to employees, including medical insurance benefits, pension benefits, company policies (such as absenteeism), and how to report various kinds of harassment. I sat with the students for the first few minutes of the meeting, then excused myself so I could leave them alone with the manager. The meeting continued for an hour or so. When it was over, the manager, who has a master's degree in business administration, reported that the students had done very well in defining the task and had raised some important points he had not considered. I was pleased to hear this, but the real satisfaction for me came on the trip home in the bus. One of my students turned to me and said, "You know, Mr. McCain, meeting with that manager to find out about the Web site really wasn't any different from when you pretend to be someone else in class." I just smiled, but inside my head I said, "Bingo!" That student had just stepped seamlessly from my classroom into a real-world business meeting and had not noticed the difference. This was exactly what I was hoping to accomplish when I set out teaching my students with the problem-solving approach outlined in this book. I have rarely felt as satisfied with my teaching as I did at that moment.

References

Armstrong, S. (Ed.). (2003). *Snapshots! Educational insights from the Thornburg Center.* Lake Barrington, IL: The Thornburg Center for Professional Development.

Bransford, J., Brown, A., & Cocking, R. (Eds.). (1999). *How people learn.* Washington, DC: National Academy Press.

Gardner, H. (1983). *Frames of mind.* New York: Basic Books.

Gates, B. (1995). *The road ahead.* Newark, NJ: Viking Press.

Hirsch, E. D. (1987). *Cultural literacy.* New York: Houghton Mifflin.

Hirsch, E. D. (1996). *The schools we need.* New York: Doubleday.

Master, D. (1999, December 7). [Keynote speech given at Southwestern Ohio Instructional Technology Association (SOITA) Conference], Dayton, OH.

More people graduate high school, college. (2004, June 29). *USA Today.* Retrieved October 8, 2004, from http://www.usatoday.com/news/education/2004-06-29-diplomas-census_x.htm

Ohler, J. (Ed.). (2001). *Future courses.* Bloomington, MN: Technos Press.

Perlman, L. (1992). *School's out.* New York: Avon Books.

Peters, T. (1986). *What gets measured gets done.* Tribune Media Services, Inc. Retrieved October 1, 2004, from http://www.tompeters.com/col_entries .php?note=005143&year=1986

Robinson, M. (2003). *What box?* Casper, WY: Natrona County Schools.

Rogers, C. (1994). *Freedom to learn.* Newark, NJ: Prentice Hall.

Schuller, B. (2000, September 29). [Address to the Educational Advisory Committee for AOL], Washington, DC.

Sousa, D. (2001). *How the brain learns.* Thousand Oaks, CA: Corwin.

Swindoll, C. (1982). *Strengthening your grip.* Waco, TX: Word Books.

Thornburg, D. (1994). *Education in the communication age.* San Carlos, CA: Starsong.

Thornburg, D. (2002). *Shift control: Reflections on education, technology, and the lives of today's students.* Lake Barrington, IL: The Thornburg Center for Professional Development.

Weinberg, G. (1985). *The secrets of consulting.* New York: Dorset House.

Wurman, R. S. (1989). *Information anxiety.* New York: Bantam Books.

Wurman, R. S. (2001). *Information anxiety 2.* Indianapolis, IN: Que.

Index

Attitude, positive, 80–81

Classroom management, 19
Confidence, 41–42
Content instruction:
    lecture-style teaching and,
        10–13, 19
    new role for teachers,
        14–15, 76–77
    providing context to, 22–26
    school skills and, 5–7
Context, power of, 22–26
Cultural Literacy (Hirsch), 6

Debrief step, in problem-solving,
    64–67, 78–79
Decision-making responsibility,
    26–28
Define step, in problem-solving,
    51–57, *56*, 78
Design step, in problem-solving,
    57–62, *60*, *62*, 78
Differentiated instruction, 58
Discovery learning, 20–21, 28
    See also Independent and higher
        learning, teaching for
Do step, in problem-solving,
    63–64, 78
4 Ds, in problem-solving:
    Debrief step, 64–67
    Define step, 51–57, *56*, 78
    Design step, 57–62, *60*, *62*, 78
    Do step, 63–64

introduction, 50–51, 84
    See also Problem-solving process

Evaluation, of personal attributes,
    79–82
Evaluation, of process skills:
    debriefing, 64–67
    new role for teachers, 77
    student evaluations, 73–75, *74*
    teacher evaluations,
        67–73, 77–79
Evaluation, reevaluation of:
    in independent and higher
        learning, 44–48

Failure, fear of, 40–44
Fear of failure, 40–44
Freedom to Learn (Rogers), 21

Gardner, H., 58
Gates, B., 42
Goal setting, 71
Grading criteria, 54

Higher education, 13–14
Hirsch, E. D., 6
How the Brain Learns (Sousa), 23

Implementing ideas, 63–64
Independent and higher learning,
    teaching for:
    fostering independent thinking,
        26–28

Page numbers in italics refer to figures.

introduction, 17–18
moving to problem solving, 28–39
progressively withdrawing from
      helping students, 39–44
providing context to content,
      22–26
reevaluating evaluation,
      44–48, 81
resisting the temptation to
      "tell," 18–21
role of technology, 35–39
shift from telling to discovery,
      31–34
transforming your curriculum,
      34–35
   See also Problem-solving process
Industrial Age workplace, 7–10
Information Anxiety 2 (Wurman), 20
Information recall, 23–24
Instructional methods. *See*
      Independent and higher
      learning, teaching for;
      Problem-solving process
Intellectual anorexia, 40
Interest in learning, role of, 20–21

Lecture-style teaching, 10–13, 19

Master, D., 24, 46
Meaning, establishing, 23–24
Memory connections, 23–24
Motivation in learning, role of, 20–21
Multiple-choice questions, 45
Multiple intelligences, 58

Personal attributes, evaluating,
      79–82
Peters, T., 45
Portfolios, 47
Postsecondary education, myth
      of, 13–14
Practice tasks, 41–42
Problem definitions, 51–57, 56
Problem-solving process:
   4 Ds in, 50–51, 75–76
   Debrief step in, 64–67
   Define step in, 51–57, 56

Design step in, 57–62, *60, 62*
Do step in, 63–64
making the transition, 82–83
putting it all together, 75–76
role of technology, 35–39
role-play approach, 28–30, 50
shift from telling to discovery,
      31–34
student evaluation of, 73–75, *74*
teacher evaluation of, 67–73,
      77–79
teaching the process, 49–50
transforming your curriculum,
      34–35
   See also Real-world problems
Process skills, student evaluation of,
      73–75, *74*
Process skills, teacher evaluation of:
   introduction, 67–68
   project design, 70–72
   project management, 69
   research, 69–70
   teamwork, 72–73
   time management, 63, 68–69
Project design skills, 70–72
Project management skills, 69

Real-world problems:
   new role for teachers, 14–15,
      76–77
   personal scenario, 3–5
   preparing for success, 84–85
   school-to-work transition and, 1–3
   in the 21st century, 7–10
   See also Independent and higher
      learning, teaching for
Research skills, 69–70
Right/wrong approach, 42–43
The Road Ahead (Gates), 42
Role-play approach:
   benefits of, 28–30, 50
   role of technology, 35–39
   shift from telling to discovery,
      31–34
   transforming your curriculum,
      34–35
   See also Problem-solving process

School skills, 5–7
School-to-work transition, 1–3
Schuller, B., 13
Self-confidence, 41–42
Self-discovered learning, 20–21, 28
   See also Independent and higher
     learning, teaching for
Self-evaluations, 64–67
Solution designs, 57–62, *60, 62*
Sousa, D., 23
"Stand and deliver" approach, to
   instruction, 10–13, 19
Standardized tests, teaching to,
   45–48
Swindoll, C., 80, 81

"Teach, test, and turf" approach, 40
Teamwork skills, 72–73

Technology change, in the
   21st century
   See also Industrial Age workplace
Technology change, new wave of,
   1–3, 35–39, 84–85
Telling method, of instruction,
   18–21, 31–34
Test scores, 45–48
Thornburg, D., 45, 46
Time management skills,
   63, 68–69
Timeline, design, 61, *62*, 63
Trial-and error approach, 27

Weinberg, G., 68
Working memory, 23–24
Written tests, 47
Wurman, R. S., 20, 40

CORWIN PRESS

The Corwin Press logo—a raven striding across an open book—represents the union of courage and learning. Corwin Press is committed to improving education for all learners by publishing books and other professional development resources for those serving the field of K–12 education. By providing practical, hands-on materials, Corwin Press continues to carry out the promise of its motto: **"Helping Educators Do Their Work Better."**